Hatfield and Axholme

Frontispiece Painting of the famous Royal Hunt, probably on Thorne Mere, 1609, by an unknown artist
By permission of the late Mr R.H. Coulman and Tyne Tees Television Ltd

Hatfield and Axholme

An Historical Review

Vernon Cory

Published by Providence Press,
Providence Place, Wardy Hill, Ely, Cambridgeshire

ISBN 0 903803 15 1 cased
ISBN 0 903803 14 3 paper

Published by Providence Press,
Providence Place, Wardy Hill, Ely, Cambridgeshire

Produced by Millennia Limited,
PO Box 20631, Hennessy Road Post Office, Hong Kong
Cover designed by Rosanne Chan
Printed and bound in Hong Kong

Contents

List of Figures and Tables

Figures

Tables

Acknowledgements

The author is indebted to the following people and organisations who have contributed information to, and helped in the compilation of, this work:

BKS Surveys Ltd, Coleraine NI
Cambridge University Collection of Air Photographs
The late Mr R.H. Coulman, and Mrs M. Coulman, Copt Hewick, Ripon
Mrs Cundall, Crowle
Mr C.D. Edgar (C.D. and B.A. Edgar), Nottingham
Dr G.D. Gaunt, British Geological Survey, Leeds
Geographia Ltd, London
Mr D.C. Gill, Director of Planning, Humberside County Council
Mr J. Goldsmith, Scunthorpe Museum and Art Gallery
Dr S.R. Haresign, Lincoln
Mr S. Houghton, Epworth Mechanics Institute
Mr and Mrs G. Hurst, Epworth
Dr Leahy, Scunthorpe Museum and Art Gallery
Leeds University, Department of Geography
Mr M. Limbert, Doncaster Museum and Art Gallery
Mr B. Metcalfe, Leeds
Mrs E.M. Mills, Belton
Mr P.T. Moore, Yorkshire Water Authority, Doncaster
Mr A.J. Norminton, Ministry of Agriculture, Fisheries and Food, Brigg
Mr T.R.W. Powell, South Ferriby
Mr Edmund Staunton, Orston, Nottingham
Mr Martin Taylor, Durham
Mr G. Trinder, Belton
Tyne Tees Television Ltd
Mrs C.M. Wilson, Museum of Lincolnshire Life, Lincoln
Mr D.I. Woodcock, Severn-Trent Water Authority, Gainsborough
Mr H.E. Woolgar, National Farmers' Union, Epworth

Figure 1 Situation of Hatfield and Axholme

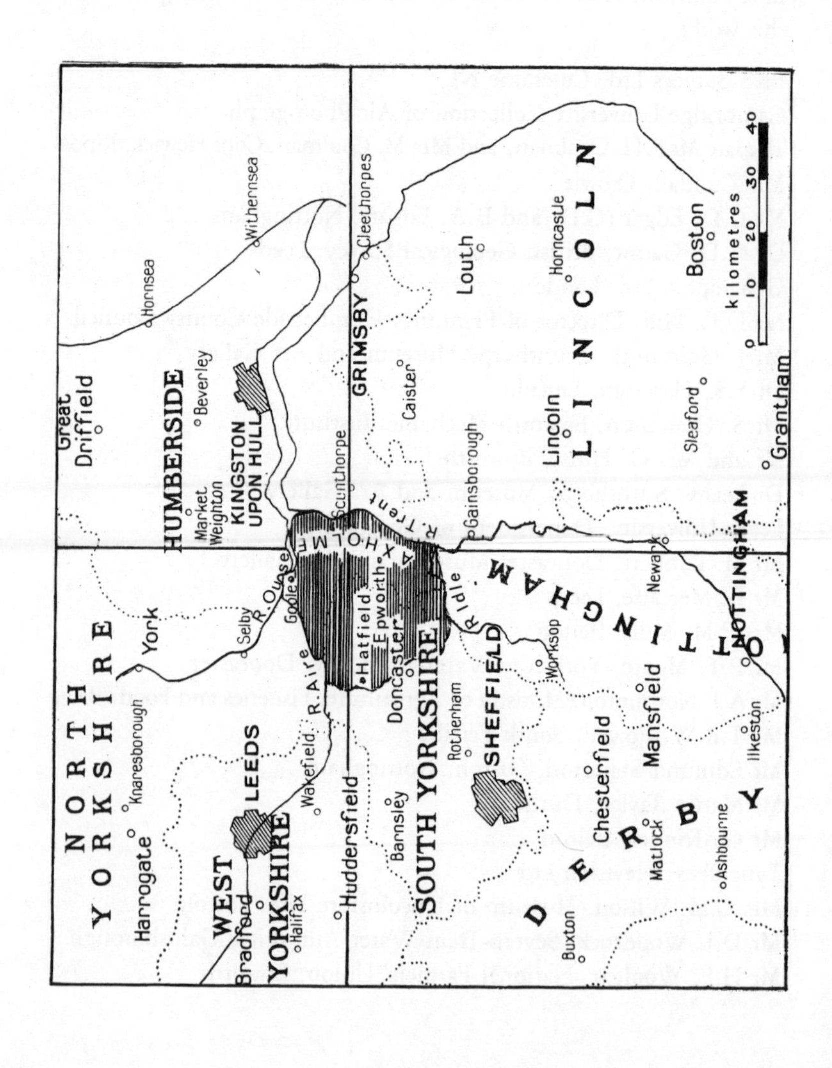

1 Introduction

Early 17th-century England relied for its wealth mainly on the products of the land. Not only did farming, together with fishing, provide almost all the staple food, but it also produced the raw materials for much home industry and for export to continental manufacturers. Similarly, forestry supplied timber for building construction, ships and even machines. Although metal working trades existed, the Industrial Revolution was still a century away.

Since time immemorial the possession of land constituted power and prosperity for kings and queens and their retinues. In turn, the rewards for war services to the crown had established the feudal lords and their great estates. Craft industries, often with strong royal encouragement, had emerged and had created a mercantile class with a firm rural base.[1] Thus there was a strong incentive to acquire more land by reclamation, resulting in the destruction of forests and the creation of farms.

Such efforts to reclaim land were limited by technical feasibility, especially attempts to recover marshland. At the beginning of the 17th century there were very substantial areas of land throughout England which were subject to temporary or permanent submersion. The larger areas included the Fens, extending from Lincoln to Cambridge, the Somerset Levels, Chat Moss in Lancashire and, in Yorkshire and Lincolnshire, Hatfield Chace and the Isle of Axholme (Figure 1). The winning of land from sea or marsh was not new and the most famous of reclaimed areas was Romney Marsh.[2] It is not known when the first enclosures of land were made in this Kentish marsh but they probably date from a pre-Roman period. Here, as elsewhere, only small areas were recovered at a time. The legal procedures for dealing with Romney land, which had evolved over time, formed the basis for the Commissions of subsequent marshland reclamations in England.

Small scale operations, often unrecorded, proceeded through the centuries but the real skill of the drainage engineer was not to become evident until the 17th century when the Dutch enjoyed their golden age of activity throughout Europe. Their first major work in England was in Hatfield Chace and its impact upon this remote and socially isolated area was both dramatic and far-reaching.

When large projects are launched in advanced countries today great efforts are made to obtain the consent of all who could possibly be affected both by the works themselves and by the expected changes in circumstances. Indeed, the strength of public opinion is capable of strangling the most ambitious of proposals. No such scruples or safeguards were recognised by Charles I and the 'contractors' employed by him, and although they had believed themselves endowed with all the necessary powers of an absolute monarchy, the rudimentary forms of democratic protest nevertheless prevailed. These protests were crude, even barbarous, although they fell a long way short of bloody revolution. During the long period of unrest the basic rule of law was maintained, despite temporary excesses. Such fundamental safeguards even withstood the stresses of the Civil Wars.

As to the drainage work itself, great tribute is due to the concept and to the breadth of vision displayed by Cornelius Vermuyden and his alien band. Less merit accrues to the planning which clearly failed to secure adequate gradients for the main channels. The main outfalls were ill chosen, inadequate provision was made for 'wash' areas, and the whole work probably suffered from the great haste with which it was conducted.

Such criticisms however must be restrained, if only because so few of the actual engineering details have been preserved. Although the literature from the post-Drainage period is abundant it tends to be scanty on technical matters, repeating the statements of others, notably those of Abraham de la Pryme.[3] The researcher would give much for the field notes of Vermuyden's engineers to discover how such a complex operation was carried out, however imperfectly.

Notes

1. Flemish weavers were attracted to England by Edward III in 1337 and cloth imports were prohibited: Smith, C.T., *Historical Geography of Western Europe before 1800* (Longman, 1978). Queen Elizabeth I took energetic measures to re-establish the cloth trade, excluded from The Netherlands trade before 1567: Trevelyan, G.M., *English Social History* (Longmans Green, 1941).
2. Dugdale, W., *History of Imbanking and Draining* (1662).
3. De la Pryme, A., *Diary* (*c.* 1698), Publication 54, Surtees Society (Thomas Jackson, 1870); and de la Pryme, A., *History and Antiquities of the Town and Parish of Hatfield* (1696), 9 volumes in MSS (British Museum, Lansdowne Collection).

2 The Extent of the Drainage Area

The area involved in the drainage and reclamation of 1626-30 included not only Hatfield Chace, which was a royal estate, but also substantial sections of the Isle of Axholme, a number of carrs and marshes to the south and 'purlieus' to the north and around the Isle.

Hatfield Chace did not have rigid boundaries, although certain reference points around the perimeter are mentioned in various accounts. An attempt to define the limits approximately is shown in Figure 2.[1] In the south, Tunnelpits, the former junction of the Rivers Torne and Idle, and Gods Cross are generally accepted as firm limits. Most accounts exclude Wroot, but that parish housed a Keeper of the Game who presumably retrieved straying game. Northwards from Gods Cross, Metcalfe lists Gunhills, Cozen Croft and Double Lidget as western markers.[2] Double Lidget, midway between Barnby Dun and Stainforth, is further east than in other accounts and it seems likely that the Chace reached the western Don near Thorpe Marsh. From here the limits extended via Hell Wicket to the confluence of the Went and the Don. As will be mentioned later, the lower part of the River Don (western arm) was almost certainly artificial and the Went extended its course eastwards at one time. It is possible that this course limited the Chace on the north side. The unmarked line passed eastwards through the quaintly named Johnny Moore Long towards Eastoft via a place, now a farm, named Boltgate. Eastoft was an important point since it boasted a Station of the Keeper of the Game.[3] From this point game straying on to the 'Northern Purlieus', and so beyond Forest Law, could be retrieved. The eastern arm of the Don formed the limits in that direction as far as Dirtness, at which point the Chace became mainly aquatic. Southwards, the island of Sandtoft housed another Keeper of the Game and the Idle itself formed the eastern margin to Tunnelpits. The whole of the Chace was within the old Yorkshire West Riding boundaries, and today the Humberside-South Yorkshire county boundary corresponds with the Gods Cross-Dirtness length of the former

Figure 2 Hatfield Chace and Epworth Manor, 1626

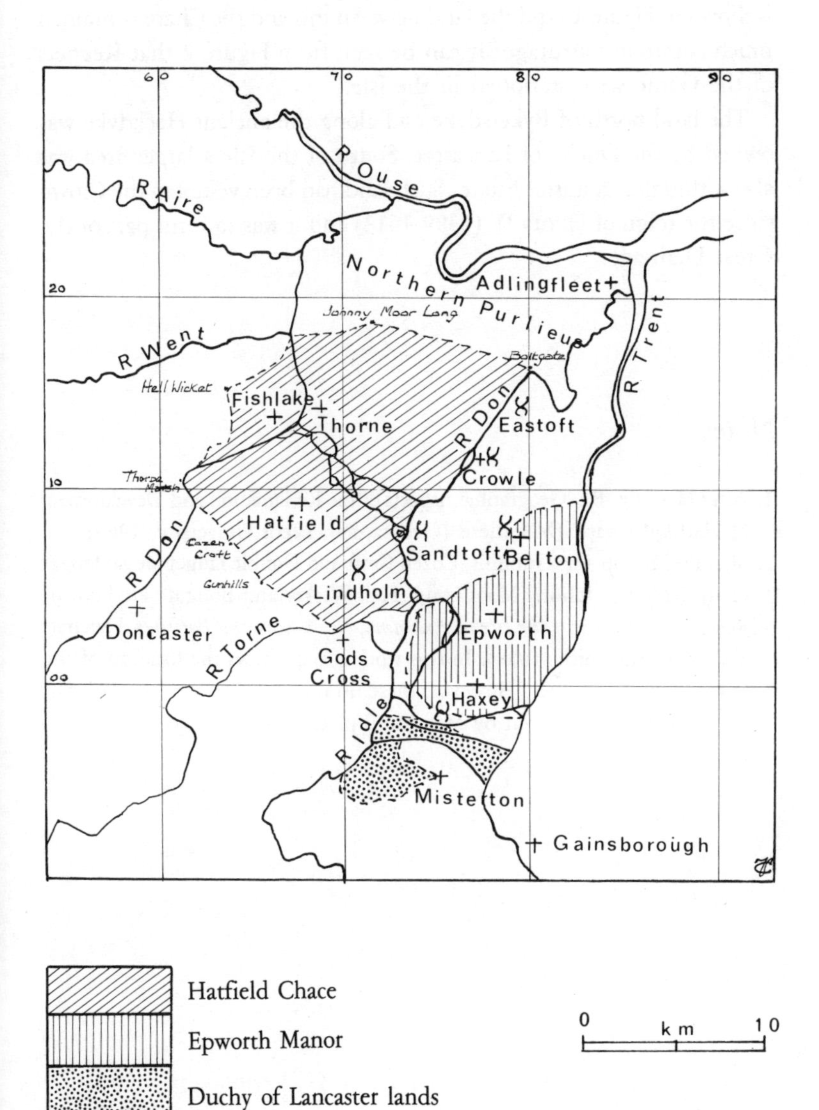

courses of the Torne and the Idle.

The considerable Manor of Epworth, including the Isle of Axholme, is shown in Figure 1, and the land between this and the Chace contained much common pasturage. It can be seen from Figure 2 that Keepers of the Game were stationed in the Isle.

The land north of Bykersdyke and along the ancient Heckdyke was owned by the Duchy of Lancaster. South of the Isle a larger area was also within the Lancaster Estate. Such land had been vested in the Crown since the reign of Henry IV (1399-1413) and it was to form part of the Great Drainage.

Notes

1. After Metcalfe, B., 'Geographic Aspects of the Reclamation and Development of Hatfield Chace' (MA thesis (Geography), Leeds University, 1960).
2. Metcalfe, B., op. cit. Gunhills, Cozen Croft and Double Lidget are no longer identifiable but Johnny Moor Long, Hell Wicket and Boltgate are known.
3. Read, W., *History of the Isle of Axholme, its Manors and Parishes*, Fletcher, T.C. (ed.) (Epworth, 1858). In this work a map shows the location of the 'Keepers of the Game'. However, these do not coincide with the 'Wards' of the five Keepers given by Metcalfe (op. cit).

3 Geographical Features

The area which includes Hatfield Chace and the Isle of Axholme resembles the Fens of Cambridgeshire to the south in several respects. Both are low-lying areas, crossed by eastward flowing rivers discharging into east coast estuaries. Both also have substantial peaty areas with 'islands' of higher land on which most of the villages are located.

The Hatfield-Axholme area is framed on the north side by the Yorkshire Ouse and on the east by the Trent. The two rivers join to form the Humber Estuary. To the west there is no sharp boundary, the land forming the southern part of the Vale of York. To the south the final reach of the River Idle approximately limits the area.

The uplands are merely low eminences, the largest being the elongated Isle of Axholme which attains a height of only 41 m. Crowle, Thorne, Hatfield, Wroot and Misterton are smaller hillocks, scarcely appearing above the main basin. Much of the land is below 3 m over OD, lower than the banks of the main rivers. The rivers and water courses are extensive and present a bewildering pattern as a result of the many changes in the drainage systems (Figure 15). The Yorkshire Ouse receives two important tributaries in the area, the Don and the Aire. The Don, rising in Grains Moss near the Derbyshire-Yorkshire border, flows east through Penistone, south into Sheffield, then northwards through Rotherham and Doncaster. Then, after a change in direction to the east, it again turns north near Thorne. At New Bridge it then takes an easterly course, known as Dutch River, to the Goole outfall.

An interesting and geologically well supported theory has been advanced by G.D. Gaunt to show that the course of the River Don between Thorne and New Bridge is a completely artificial waterway.[1] All the rivers draining to the Humber early in the post-glacial period incised their courses deeply and then filled these channels with alluvium which subsequently spread beyond the channels to form wide floodplains. Both a deeply incised 'buried' channel and a wide floodplain are conspicuously absent in the Don north of Thorne. Furthermore, Gaunt has shown that the River Went formerly extended eastwards and northwards in a manner which could not have occurred if the Don had then followed its present line. Today the Went joins the Don but its confluence must be controlled by a sluice. The old name for this stretch of the Don was Turnbrigg Dyke, which also suggests an artificial channel. The date when the dyke was cut and the name of the person who conceived the far-sighted project remain a mystery. It is known from medieval maps that the river was in its present alignment during the early 15th century, but firm dating is extremely difficult. In the light of this highly probable theory, the original course of the Don was the silty channel which reached the Trent near Adlingfleet. Until 1974 the line of the old Don in this vicinity was the county boundary between Yorkshire (West Riding) and Lincolnshire.

The Aire, the most southerly of the Dales rivers, rises near Malham in the central Pennines and passes through Skipton, Keighley and Leeds. A meandering river, its channel becomes even more contorted before traversing Snaith and Rawcliffe to join the Ouse at Airmyn. The two other principal rivers of the basin are tributaries of the Trent: the Torne and the Idle. The Torne rises near Maltby in South Yorkshire and for much of its course is contained in artificial channels. It is a slow moving river, retained by heavy embanking across Hatfield Chace. Along with a number of dykes and drains in the central area the Torne delivers its waters to the main pumping station at Keadby and so into the tidal Trent. The Idle emerges from the junction of several streams south of Retford, Nottinghamshire. It follows a meandering course through the plain and formerly continued northwards to join the Torne at Tunnelpits. Today, it turns easterly at Idle Stop, discharging into the Trent with the help of the major pumping station at West Stockwith. As in the case of the Don, the final stretch of the Idle is probably wholly artificial. The ancient name applied to this reach was Bykersdyke (variously spelled) and some early writers associate its origin with the reign of Edward III (1327-77).[2] There is no firm evidence, historical or geological, for this, but Vermuyden certainly enlarged the course to receive the whole of the Idle flow. The lower stretches of the river are heavily protected by barrier banks.

The River Trent is of outstanding significance to the region. One of Britain's longest rivers, it rises west of the Pennines in Staffordshire, at Biddulph Moor, and the distance from there to its confluence with the Humber at Trent Falls is 275 km. However, it is the character of its lower, tidal course that has shaped the development of the Hatfield-Axholme area.

The Trent is tidal up to Cromwell Weir, a distance of almost 85 km.[3] The lower tidal reach, that is the length where tidal reversal is most prominent, is the 41.8 km from the outfall to Gainsborough. The interaction of fresh, fluvial water and salt tidal water has important results. At Keadby fresh water entering the river at major flood raises high water level by 0.39 m and low water level by 1.8 m. Further upstream the corresponding high water level at Gainsborough is raised by fresh water influx by 2.35 m and the low water level by 5.18 m. Furthermore, the effect of the estuary causes levels in the river to be higher than on the coast. High spring tide at Butterwick may be 1.37 m higher than at Grimsby.[4] Flooding has been a frequent hazard through the ages and has been the cause of a number of major disasters (Table 1).[5]

Table 1 Major floods in the Lower Trent and its vicinity

1329	Morton Bank (near Gainsborough) breached. Walkerith and Stockwith flooded
1346	Extent unknown
1378	Tidal flood, widespread in Trent valley
1485/6	River frozen and Newark Bridge destroyed
1600	Extent unknown
1677	Extent unknown
1680	Extent unknown
1681	Tidal flood, extensive in lower tidal reach
1682	Breach in bank near Thorne (River Don)
1683/4	River frozen, bridges destroyed inland
1686	May floods in Rivers Idle and Eau
1689	October floods (River Idle)

1692	Extent unknown
1696	Breach near Thorne (River Don)
1697	Morton Bank breached, Dutch River, Bykersdyke affected, also Kirk Bramwith, Fishlake, Stainforth and Thorne flooded
1700/1	Thorne (River Don)
1706	Thorne
1763/4	Floods leading to Smeaton's inspection
1770	Major flood involving Hatfield Chace and lower Isle of Axholme, following breaches in Bykersdyke and Trent banks
1792	Extent unknown
1795	Morton Bank etc. and Lincoln City flooded
1797	Extent unknown
1824	Torksey Bank breached
1828	Sluices at Keadby, Snow Sewer etc. closed for weeks
1852	Above Gainsborough
1854	Details not available
1875	River Idle area. Nottingham: 13 drowned
1901	Localised damage
1910	Gainsborough and River Idle
1921	Localised damage
1932	Localised damage
1946	Extent localised
1947	Morton and Snow Sewer floodbank. Everton and Misterton Carrs (mainly east bank)
1953	Flood due to tidal surge with north-west winds. Butterwick to Gunness, also at Gainsborough

Source: After Trent River Board Report (1960, see Note 3).

The phenomenon of the Eagre is associated with the funnel-shaped channel of the lower Trent. It consists of a wave attaining a maximum height of 1.5-1.8 m which travels a distance of some 56 km up the Trent. It is caused by salt water pushing back fresh water and passing underneath in a wedge-like form. The Severn Bore is of similar origin.

The present-day drainage system is described in Chapter 21. Of the many dykes involved some are very old. Many of these, such as Paupers Drain, between Crowle and the Trent, and Snow Sewer which runs from

The River Torne at Tunnelpits. The raised artificial course was originally cut by Vermuyden. The lower level course is the soak dyke.

Tunnelpits Pumping Station, built in 1962 to take low-level water into the Torne from north and south of the river.

Aerial photograph of Idle Stop and the area near the present River Idle, 1973
By permission of Cambridge University Committee for Aerial Photography

Key to 1973 aerial photograph
The rectangular field enclosures correspond with the original Participants' lands

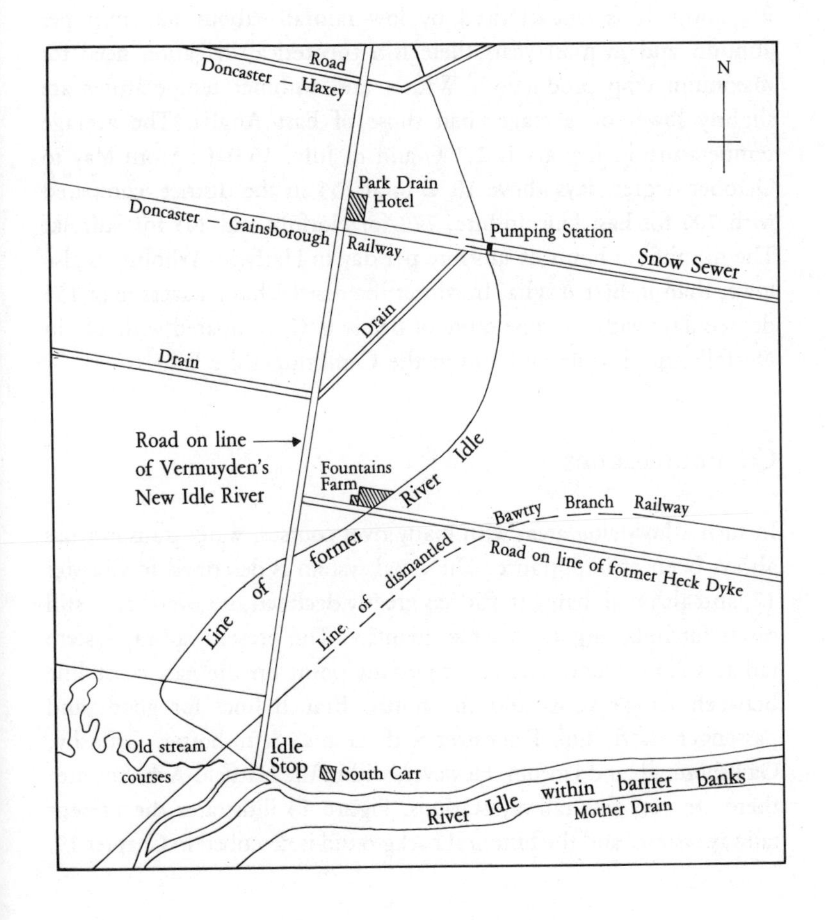

near Fountains Farm to Owston Ferry, were used for warping purposes (see Chapter 18) in the 19th century. Substantial warping on the south bank of the Yorkshire Ouse necessitated many specialised drains to convey the tidal waters. Many of these were filled in after use. The largest of these to remain is the Swinefleet Warping Drain, some 8 km in length.

Climate

The climate of the area corresponds with that of much of eastern England.[6] It is characterised by low rainfall, about 622 mm per annum, and in most years there is a theoretical irrigation need for maximum crop production. Winter and summer temperatures are slightly lower on average than those of East Anglia. The average temperature in January is 2.7 °C and in July, 16.0 °C. From May to October degree days above 10 °C total 755 in the district, compared with 705 for East Lincolnshire, 770 for Norfolk and 805 for Suffolk. The number of hours of sunshire per day in Hatfield-Axholme is also lower than in East Anglia. In winter the district has an average of 155 degree days with a temperature of below 0 °C, compared with 145 in Norfolk and Suffolk and 140 in the Cambridgeshire Fens.

Communications

In such a low-lying area, with many river courses, water transport has always been of importance. The canal system is described in Chapter 12, and although barge traffic has greatly declined, it nevertheless still caters for bulk cargoes in some quantity. The present railway system radiates from Doncaster, an important point on the east coast line between King's Cross and the north. Branch lines for goods and passenger traffic link Doncaster with Goole, Scunthorpe, Grimsby, Gainsborough and Lincoln. However, within the Hatfield-Axholme area there are very few railway stations. Figure 13 illustrates the present railway system, and the historical background is described in Chapter 19.

While railway and canal facilities have declined road transport across the area has become more important. Motorway extensions include the M 62 (Pontefract-Hull section), the M 18 (Rawcliffe-Sheffield section) and the M 180 (Thorne-Scunthorpe-Grimsby section). The trunk roads A 161 (running north-south through the Isle of Axholme), A 18 (west-east, Thorne to Scunthorpe) and A 614 (Knottingley-Goole) link with the motorways and with the main 'artery', the Great North Road (A 1), to provide excellent road transport facilities.

Industry

With the Industrial Revolution heavy industry was established at Doncaster and, somewhat later, at Scunthorpe, both on the periphery of the area. In Doncaster coal mining, railway engineering, glass making and manufacturing attracted labour from the surrounding districts which included Hatfield-Axholme. Iron mining, followed by steel making, characterised Scunthorpe, which, similarly, acted as a focus for the local agricultural labour. The town of Thorne developed from the time of the improvements to the River Don.[7] In 1882 it was written that: 'Probably there did not exist a score of dwellings where the modern town of Thorne now principally stands until Vermuyden had thrown up that huge bank from Ashfield to Simon Houses.'[8] To the agricultural and peat digging pursuits were added small ship building and engineering in the 19th century. In the present century coal mining was begun and later discontinued at Moorends, Thorne. The Hatfield-Stainforth colliery has continued in production. Goole's prosperity started soon after it was chosen as the outfall point for Dutch River.[9] With a close connection, at first by water and later by rail and road, with the West Yorkshire industrial areas it provided facilities for exports and imports, mainly using coastal shipping.

Bawtry on the River Idle also benefited from the enlargement of Dutch River and from the shortened connection with Trent and Humber which Vermuyden provided. By the mid-18th century the proximity of Bawtry to Sheffield resulted in a considerable increase in the commercial importance of Bawtry. Flat-bottomed craft of up to 200 tonnes burden were used to load wrought-iron, lead, tools, millstones and heavy goods from Sheffield for onward shipment.

Whereas village inhabitants were once attracted away from their homes to more lucrative employment in the surrounding towns, the increase in personal transport had caused the pendulum to swing back by the 1960s. Hatfield and Axholme have increasingly become 'dormitories' for industrial and administrative workers.

Though now employing fewer persons than ever before, agriculture is still of considerable importance in the area (see Chapter 22). Fishing has long ceased to be of economic importance, although the sport of coarse fishing is extremely popular with enthusiasts from near and far.

Notes

1. Gaunt, G.D., 'The artificial nature of the River Don north of Thorne, Yorkshire', *Yorkshire Archaeological Journal*, No. 47 (1975), pp. 15-21.
2. 'Bykersdyke or "Bicker...", Old Scandinavian - "village marsh" ' in Ekwall, E., *Concise Oxford Dictionary of English Place-Names* (Oxford, 1959).
3. Nixon, M., 'Report on Tidal Reach Improvement Plan' (Trent River Board, 1960).
4. Trent River Board Report, 1960, op. cit.
5. Willis, W.R., 'Historic Floods in the Isle of Axholme and Hatfield', *Durdey's Almanack and General Advertiser* (1901); and Radley, J. and Simms, C., *Yorkshire Flooding*, Sessions of York.
6. Smith, L.P., *Agricultural Climate* (HM Stationery Office, 1976).
7. Casson, M., *History of Thorne* (1869).
8. Tomlinson, J., *The Level of Hatfield Chace and Parts Adjacent* (1882).
9. British Transport Board, *150 Years of the Port of Goole* (1976).

4 Geology, Soils and Minerals

Triassic rocks form the bedrock throughout the Hatfield-Axholme area (Table 2). They consist of Sherwood (ex-Bunter) Sandstone west of a line from Goole to Misson, dipping eastwards beneath the Mercia Mudstone (ex-Keuper) Marl.[1] The upstanding nature of the Isle of Axholme (Figure 3) and the hills of Crowle and Misterton is due to the hard, resistant, gypsiferous Clarborough Beds within the Mercia Mudstone.

Considerable erosion took place during the Tertiary and early

Figure 3 Geological section

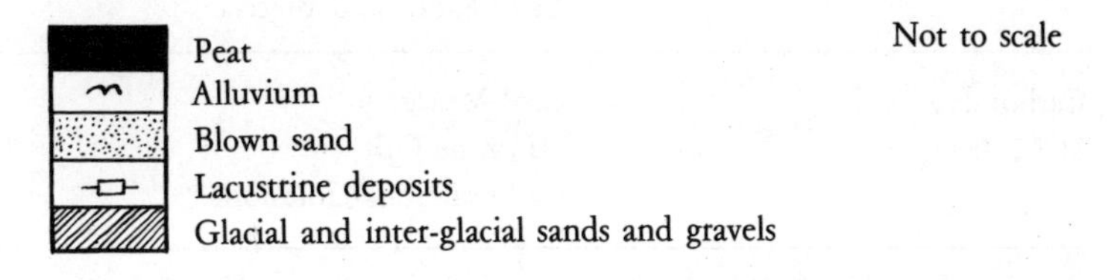

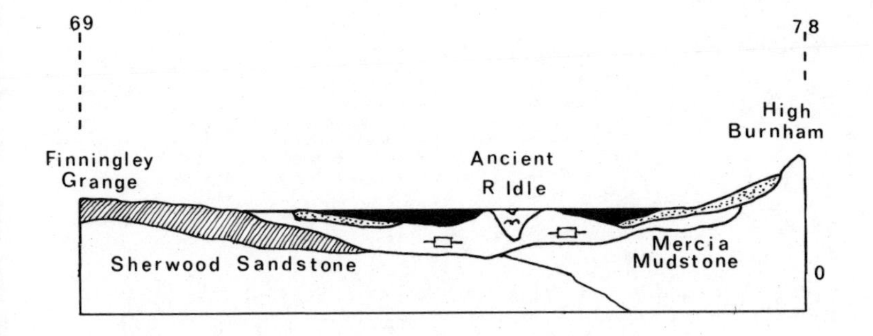

Table 2 Rocks and deposits of the Hatfield-Axholme area

System and approximate age in my (millions of years)	Rocks and deposits
Quaternary (up to 2.2 my)*	Flandrian (post-glacial) deposits Devensian (last-glacial) deposits Ipswichian (last-interglacial) deposits Pre-Ipswichian (older glacial) deposits
Trias 250-205 my	Mercia Mudstone Sherwood Sandstone
Permian 290-250 my	Upper Marl Upper Magnesian Limestone Middle Marl Lower Magnesian Limestone Lower Marl Marl Slate Basal Sands and Breccia
Carboniferous 365-290 my	Coal Measures Millstone Grit Carboniferous Limestone

*No deposits in the Hatfield-Axholme area are older than 0.7 million years.

Source: G.D. Gaunt

Quaternary periods when any pre-existing Jurassic and Cretaceous rocks were removed and the principal valleys draining the surrounding uplands (the Aire, Don, Trent, etc.) were forming. Subsequently, a sequence of cold glacial and warm interglacial episodes affected the region.[2] Gravels and clays from an earlier glaciation cap the Sherwood Sandstone ridges at Doncaster and Rossington, and Ipswichian (last) interglacial sand and gravel spreads cover much of the ground around Hatfield Woodhouse, Finningley and Misson.

During the Devensian (last) glaciation ice entered the region only briefly and to the north-east of Wroot.[3] For much of this glacial phase the region lay submerged beneath a lake ('Lake Humber') produced by glacial blockage across the Humber gap (Figure 4). The laminated clays formed in this lake are responsible for the flat topography of much of the region. After the lake drained, blown sand accumulated in places, particularly on the west-facing slopes of the Isle of Axholme during a final cold phase. With scrub clearance in historic times some of the blown sand again became prone to Aeolian action (Figure 3). During early post-glacial times a warmer and fairly dry (Boreal) climate enabled the growth of thick vegetation with widespread woodland, a fact evinced by pollen analysis.

By the Late Bronze Age some woodland had been cleared to the extent needed to establish settlements, and carbonised residues indicate that the trees may have been burned off. However, this dry period was followed by wetter conditions with a rise in tide levels off the east coast. 'Buried' forests on the Lincolnshire coast and at some inland sites confirm this marine inundation. At the same time rivers started to form clayey, alluvial floodplains along their courses. Waterlogging, at first with alkaline ground water, gave rise to fen peats. This was overtaken by wetter conditions favouring *Sphagnum* and *Eriophorum* development. Rainfall at this time was around 1,500 mm, comparable to that of western mountainous districts in Britain today. This 'hochmor' or raised bog formation originated without the customary reed swamp phase. On Hatfield Moor the bog probably succeeded a pine forest that had developed during the previous dry (Boreal) phase. The hochmor degenerated only to be succeeded by a series of three more flooding phases, each marked by *Scheuzeria* moss growth.[4]

Figure 4 Lake Humber, late Devensian Phase

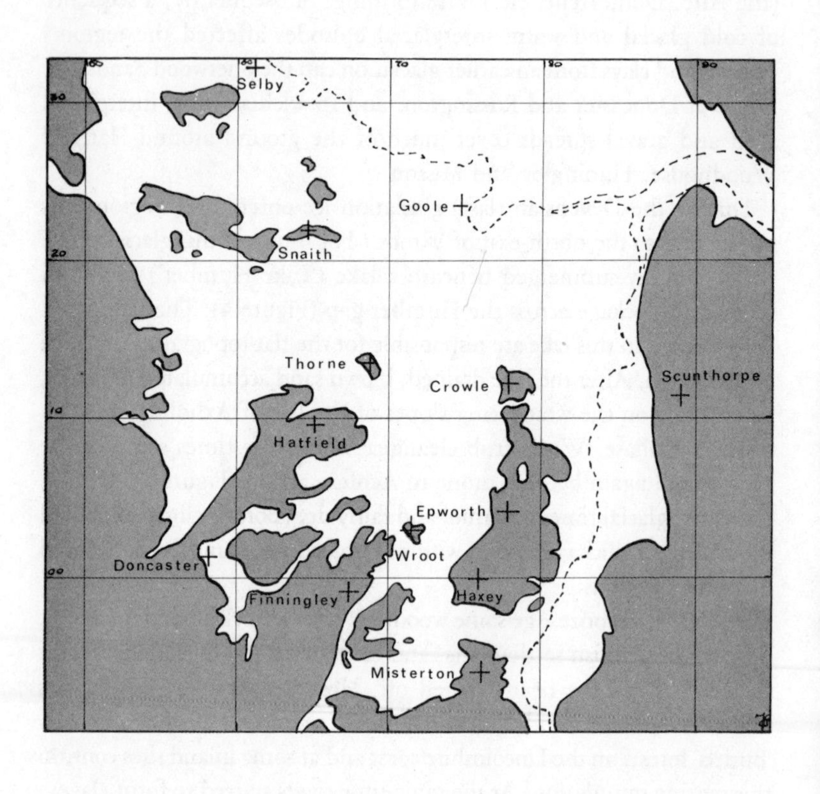

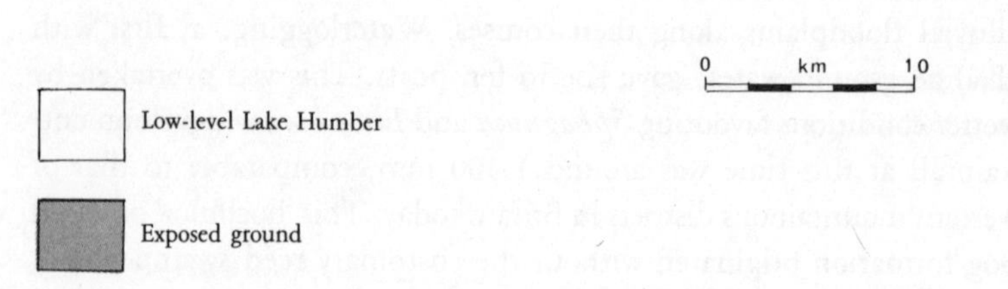

Source: G.D. Gaunt

The soils produced by the hochmor peat are classified by the Soil Survey of England and Wales as of the 'Longmoss' series. The series is characterised by remaining undrained and permanently wet and acid. Over appreciable areas upper layers of raw peat have been removed by cutting. In the farmed areas lying between the Hatfield Moors and the Isle of Axholme the fen peat soil is classified within the 'Adventurers" series. This soil is alkaline or neutral and is mainly under artificial drainage control, that is, pumped. Despite some risk of blowing it is a highly fertile medium especially for root crops. A few areas are undrained.

With regard to minerals, gypsum and anhydrite are found in the Mercia Mudstone in the Isle of Axholme and were utilised from medieval times. Leland, writing in 1538, describes the plentiful quantities of 'alabaster', some of which, he states, was hard enough for building stone.[5] It was used extensively as flooring material and even formed the foundations of large buildings. The presence of fossil fuels underlying the region was only first suspected late in the 19th century. The Upper Carboniferous Coal Measures dip under the Permo-Triassic strata. In 1893 a diamond drilling made at South Carr, near Idle Stop, revealed the Shafton Seam at 580 m and the thick Barnsley Seam at 914 m.[6] Interest in establishing a colliery was greatly encouraged by this finding and plans were made by a German Company to sink a shaft.[7] With commendable foresight, catering for the thirsts of the intended miners was regarded as of the highest priority. Thus a substantial hotel was immediately erected in the deserted levels of Westwoodside. The year was 1914 and the promoter's plans received a sharp reverse with the outbreak of the First World War. So it was that the welcoming edifice of Park Drain Hotel received the nickname of 'Klondyke' from its local devotees!

Later, collieries were developed at Hatfield and at Thorne, although the latter mine is not in production at present. It is likely that in the future these deep reserves will be exploited. Already the major coalfield near Selby, only just outside the area, is being developed. The Coal Measures are the source of natural gas in the North Sea exploitation, with the gas being trapped in the Lower Permian Sands (Rotliegendes). As recently as 1981-2 trial borings revealed gas at Lindholme.

Notes

1. For further geological information, see Edwards, W. and Trotter, F.M., 'The Pennines and Adjacent Areas' (1968); Kent, P., Gaunt, G.D. and Wood, C.J., 'Eastern England from the Tees to the Wash' (HMSO, Institute of Geological Sciences, 1980); and Geological Sheets, 1:50,000, No. 79 (Goole) and No. 88 (Doncaster).
2. Gaunt, G.D., 'Quaternary history of the southern part of the Vale of York', in Neale, J. and Flenley, J. (eds), *The Quaternary in Britain* (Pergamon Press, London and New York, 1981), pp. 82-97.
3. Gaunt, G.D., 'The Devensian maximum ice limit in the Vale of York', *Proceedings of the Yorkshire Geological Society*, Vol. 40 (1976), pp. 631-7.
4. Smith, A.G., 'Post-glacial Deposits in South Yorkshire and North Lincolnshire', *New Phytologist*, Vol. 57 (1958), pp. 19-49.
5. Smith, L.T., *The Itinerary of John Leland (1534-1543)* (1906/1910).
6. Dunston, G., *The Rivers of Axholme* (A. Brown and Sons, ?1909).
7. Hugo Stinnes, a German coal magnate, had purchased all rights to develop the site. At this time a syndicate was also seeking a lease on Belton Grange Farm for coal mining development: Korthals-Altes, J., *Sir Cornelius Vermuyden* (Williams and Norgate and W.P. Van Stockum, 1925).

5 The Ancient History of the Area

Almost nothing is known of events and people of the central area before Roman times. It is believed that extensive deforestation took place from the Bronze Age onwards. Evidence for this is shown by the relics of abundant beetle species which were associated with decaying timber. According to Buckland, primeval forest in this area disappeared 2,000 years ago.[1] It is probable that Bronze Age settlements were established over much of the Hatfield Chace and Axholme region at this time since dry conditions then obtained.

The remaining peat moors of Thorne and Hatfield provide valuable information on previous conditions in the whole area. Smith found indications in pollen analysis from Hatfield Moor of early neolithic agriculture (*c.* 4000 BC).[2] Archaeologists are of the opinion that many sites lie buried beneath peat deposits, awaiting discovery.

Scattered items from the Bronze Age have been recovered. Amongst these, and on view at the Scunthorpe Museum, are a Tara torque from Low Burnham and a fine jadeite axe found at Wroot but probably of eastern European origin.

Abraham de la Pryme, sometime Curate of Hatfield and Vicar of Thorne, writing in 1698 and describing the history of the area, gives an account of conflict between the British Briganti and the Romans.[3] In this he states that forests of the area gave cover to the British tribesmen who were thereby enabled to harass the invaders. The Romans allegedly burned down the forests and later flooded the land in order to control the troublesome natives. Blackened trunks found in more recent times were thought to confirm this story. However there is no evidence whatever to support the statements, and it is now generally attributed to the Vicar's fertile imagination!

There is no doubt that extensive forests grew in the region at times, but with inundations peat developed, killing the trees and at the same time preserving them *in situ*. A similar sequence occurred in many low-lying areas throughout Britain and so-called bog oaks are commonly encountered in cultivations in the Lincolnshire and Cambridgeshire Fens. In 1662 Dugdale described buried trees in the Hatfield Chace and quoted the peasantry as removing as many as 2,000 cartloads in a single year.[4]

The main Roman invasion commenced in AD 43. It was led by Aulus Platius for the Emperor Claudius and there was a steady penetration and absorption of local populations. Strong resistance was offered the invaders by the northern Briganti and by the Parisi of East Yorkshire. Austerfield or Finningley may have been the site of a battle where the Britons were defeated in AD 61. Romano-British relics have been found generally throughout the area although traces of settlement sites are limited. Stable Roman occupation would seem to have been concentrated on Doncaster. Roman forces appear to have moved up the Vale of York on the west and via the Lincolnshire Wolds to the Humber on the east, leaving the marshy, impenetrable area in the centre. The region was almost certainly not a Brigantian base, since this British tribe utilised mountain top fortresses. Further south Belgic Celts made use of swampy areas, such as those around Colchester, for defence.

Doncaster (Danum) was the most important Roman city in the southern Vale of York, and numerous relics of the long occupation have been found beneath the modern town.[5] Probably, the Romano-British settlements gradually developed into concentrated villages with infield and outfield, as subsequent invaders integrated with the population. Place names provide interesting clues to the origins of post-Roman settlements.[6] A number of these have strong Scandinavian associations, such as Haxey, Axholme, Keadby, Sandtoft and Eastoft. Others are of mixed Old English and Scandinavian ancestry, such as Hatfield, Stainforth, Snaith and Owston. Purely Old English (which implies Anglo-Saxon) are Thorne, Fishlake, Sykehouse, Idle, Butterwick, Wroot, Adlingfleet, Crowle and Luddington.

The first waves of these incoming peoples were Anglo-Saxons. After their initial landings, which had started even before the departure of the Roman legions, the invaders had fanned out over the whole of England. They became integrated with the indigenous peoples and gradually distinctive and rival kingdoms emerged. Hatfield and Axholme lay in Mercia, near the boundary between that kingdom and that of Northumbria to the north of the Humber. Thus its position somewhat resembled that of Flanders, where armies clashed in frontier battles.

Bede, in his *Historica Ecclesiastica,* refers to Axholme in reference to two battles in that area. One of these took place in AD 617 near the River Idle when Raewald, King of the East Angles, defeated and killed Aethelfrith, King of Northumbria, and placed Eadwine, whom he had been sheltering, on the throne of a reunited Northumberland. This same Eadwine founded the city of Edinburgh by building there the original fortress. He also introduced Christianity as the established religion.

However, after a hectic and successful period of conquest, Eadwine was challenged by the forces of Penda, King of Mercia. In 633 Penda's army, augmented by allies from North Wales, overcame Eadwine and his men at Hatfield, on the site of Eadwine's 'palace'.[7] Eadwine himself was killed, and Penda's position and prestige were greatly strengthened. Penda again attacked the Northumbrians in 642 and in battle, Oswald King of Northumbria, was killed. The site of the battle has not been precisely located, but a long established legend connects Oswald with the Isle of Axholme. Oswald had embraced Christianity and had acquired something of the aura of a saint by his general demeanour. Thus it is that the churches of Crowle and Althorpe are dedicated to this Northumbrian king.

Penda was finally defeated in 655 by Oswin of Bernicia (part of Northumbria) at a battle near the present-day city of Leeds. His death marked the formal adoption of Christianity by the Kingdom of Mercia.

In the struggles for supremacy between the Anglo-Saxon kingdoms the Hatfield-Axholme area does not receive specific mention in the following centuries. It was not until the coming of the Normans that the area re-entered the annals of history. In the intervening period, however, the rivers and estuaries felt the full impact of the last Viking invasions. During the 8th and 9th centuries raiding parties penetrated the Humber, Ouse and Trent and established themselves at certain points, including York and Gainsborough. At Gainsborough, Sweyn assumed the title of 'King'. The unsuccessful attempts to dislodge the Vikings by Ethelred, the Saxon King, and by his successor, Edmund Ironside, culminated in the crowning of Sweyn's son Cnut, as King of all England. A marked degree of integration of the Vikings and the Saxons took place in this part of England. This is shown by a remarkable event after the Norman Conquest. The King of Denmark entered the Humber with an army in 1068, and, seeking the help of local inhabitants, he threatened the Norman King with invasion. Strategically poised near Adlingfleet, the Danes constituted a formidable force and William found himself with no alternative but to buy off the attack with a substantial 'Danegeld'. With this settlement, not unfamiliar to the Danes, the insurgents returned home.

Soon after the Conquest William instituted the great Domesday survey and its contents provide us with a monumental account of civilisation in Anglo-Saxon England.

For the Hatfield-Axholme area the following record of arable land within the Manor of Conisburgh is given in the survey:[8]

Stainforth,	3 carucates [146 ha, 360 acres]
Fishlake,	5 carucates [243 ha, 600 acres]
Thorne,	4 carucates [194 ha, 480 acres]
Tudworth,	1 carucate [48 ha, 120 acres]
Hatfield,	8 carucates [388 ha, 960 acres]

Details are given of plough teams and these indicate that the intensity of cultivation in these townships in the Hatfield district was considerably less than in the Isle of Axholme and the rest of Lincolnshire. The lists of taxes paid suggest that Stainforth was the most fertile township, although Fishlake supported a higher population. Townships east of the Don tended to be less prosperous than those to the west.

Two centuries later the 1379 Poll Tax supplies an indication of local populations:

Hatfield	£123	Hook	£42
Stainforth	£67	Ousefleet	£78
Haldenby	£118	Fockerby	£50
(Luddington)		Adlingfleet	£92
Whitgift	£55	Airmyn	£148
Thorne	£171	Snaith	£275
Fishlake	£157	Rawcliffe	£222
Reedness	£135		

Domesday also recorded 20 fisheries at Tudworth (near Thorne, but now a vanished village) where each farm contributed 1,000 eels annually to the Lord of the Manor. There were also fisheries at Thorne and Whitgift.

The above townships formed part of the fee of Conisbrough during the reign of King Harold.[9] At the Conquest this area was awarded by William I to his son-in-law William de Warenne, who was made Earl of Surrey. Included in the area was the Chace of Hatfield. In its original spelling a chace, in Middle English and in Old French, referred to unenclosed parkland in private ownership. This description exactly fitted the Hatfield hunting forest. This spelling is therefore retained by the author, although the Corporation employs 'chase' and general usage has tended to outmode 'chace'. However, in 1626 it was so spelled. Upon the death of de Warenne in 1347 the Chace reverted to the Crown.

Earlier, in 1331, de Warenne had been given the right to 'approve' wastes in both Thorne and Hatfield Moors. 'Approvement' is the authority to enclose superfluous wastelands as defined in the Commons Acts of 1235 and 1285. After some 170 ha (421 acres) had been so taken the right was challenged successfully and the land was restored by the Crown to its original state. Not until the 19th century were enclosures restarted, though turf cutters reclaimed 'graved' peat lands after digging in Thorne Moors.

In the Isle of Axholme William of Normandy conferred a large area upon Geoffrey de Wirce. Subsequently the award was transferred during the reign of Henry I (1100-35) to Nigel d'Albini, who had been 'Bow Bearer' to William Rufus. His successor took the name 'Mowbray' and from this root the Duchy of Norfolk directly derives. The Mowbray seat was Kinnaird Castle at Owston Ferry, a small Trentside market town.[10]

At the Conquest this area included the manors of Epworth and Westwood, Belton, Haxey, Beltoft, Owston, Crowle, Althorpe, Luddington, Burnham and Wroot, as well as Blyborough, Somerby, Solethorpe, Gainsborough and Lound lying outside the Isle. In time, the Mowbrays set up a Manor Court at Epworth which, incorporating a Court Leet, constituted a powerful centre of jurisdiction. This Court extended its remit so as to embrace much of the Isle of Axholme, while retaining the title of the Manor of Epworth. The map in Figure 2 shows approximately the district covered.

During the reign of Henry VII the manor passed to the Earl of Derby, who had married the last female representative of the House of Mowbray. It became Crown property in Elizabethan times but in 1649 Charles II (although not the lawful king at that time) granted the manor to Sir George Carteret on lease for 90 years. During the Civil Wars the Court appeared to have become defunct but the rolls were later fortuitously restored, at least to a nominal extent, following a renewal of the lease. In 1856 Read reports George Spofforth Lister, of Hirst Priory, as becoming Lord of the Manor of Epworth.[11] However, by this time many of the ancient functions of the Court had been superseded by modern courts and assizes.

Hatfield Chace became a royal property in 1374 when it passed from the domain of the Earls of Surrey to the House of York. However it did not become subject to Forest Law until 1460, at the time of the accession of Edward IV.

Henry VIII appears never to have found time to hunt in the Chace, though on at least one occasion considerable preparations were made for him to do so. He did not lack interest since, in 1541, the monastic estate of Roche Abbey at Armthorpe and that of Selby Abbey at Crowle Manor were added to the Chace following the Dissolution of the Monasteries.

Notes

1. Buckland, P.C. and Kenward, H.K., 'Thorne Moor, a Paleo-ecological Study of a Bronze Age Site', *Nature*, Vol. 241 (1973), pp. 405-6.
2. Smith, A.G., 'Post Glacial Deposits in South Yorkshire and North Lincolnshire', *New Phytologist*, Vol. 57 (1958), pp. 19-49.
3. De la Pryme, A., *Diary* (*c.* 1698), op. cit.
4. Dugdale, W. (1662), op. cit.
5. Magilton, J.R., *Doncaster District, an Archaeological Survey* (Doncaster Museum, 1977); and Hatfield, C.W., *Historical Notices of Doncaster* (1866).
6. Ekwall, E. (1959), op. cit.
7. Peck, W., *A Topographical History and Description of Bawtry and Thorne*

and Villages Adjacent (printed by Thomas and Hunsley, 1813/14). There is doubt as to the precise location of this battle. Haethfelth (*c.* 730, Old English (Bede), see Ekwall, E., op. cit.) was assumed to refer to Hatfield, Yorkshire in older histories (e.g., Gardner, S.R. (1898)) but one rival site has been suggested at Warsop, Nottinghamshire, and there may be others.

8. Page, W. (ed.), *Victoria History of County of York*, Vol. 2 (1912).
9. Metcalfe, B. (1960), op, cit.
10. Loughlin, N. and Miller, K.R., 'Survey of Archaeological Sites in Humberside' (Humberside Joint Archaeological Committee, 1980). Kinnaird Castle was a Norman motte and bailey castle which was refortified by Roger de Mowbray during the revolt against Henry II in 1173-4. It was destroyed in 1174 and was not rebuilt. The church and churchyard are built over one of the two baileys. The motte and south bailey ditches survive but are overgrown.
11. Read, W. (1858), op. cit.

6 The Mowbray Award

Of the several aristocratic houses associated with the Isle of Axholme the Mowbrays occupied the paramount position until late Tudor times. Nigel d'Albini inherited the estates of Robert Mowbray (his uncle), as well as acquiring the possessions of Geoffrey de Wirce. His loyalty to Henry I had been rewarded by enormous land grants: 12 lordships in Warwickshire, 27 in Leicestershire and 24 in Lincolnshire, including the before-mentioned Epworth and associated manors. Of his two sons, Roger took the name of Mowbray and the succession during the next two centuries was as follows:

Roger de Mowbray (living in 1145)	A notable benefactor of religious houses, establishing Byland Abbey and Newburgh Priory *inter alia*. He was also closely associated with the Knights Templar Order.
Nigel (died 1191)	Died on his way to the Crusades.
William (died 1222)	Involved in the Magna Carta issue.
Roger (died 1266)	Said to be 'fond of domestic ease'.
Roger (died 1298)	Buried in Fountains Abbey.
John	Hanged at York for treason and his estates confiscated, 1321.
John (died 1368)	Famed for the Mowbray Award (or 'Deed').

In addition to the Mowbray Castle at Kinnaird (Owston Ferry) the family owned a mansion at Epworth, known as Vine Garth. It was here that the last named John de Mowbray was born and his action was to become vitally important to the Axholme inhabitants more than 250 years later.

Although loyalty to the Crown was not a consistent feature of the Mowbrays, John retained his father's close relationship with Edward III. He was at Edward's side during the battle of Crécy (1346) and took part in the peace settlement with the French King. At home he was clearly a good landlord, sensitive to the rights of his tenants. It was in this respect that he acknowledged grievances which had been occasioned by his own acquisition of common land. As a result he established a legal charter, largely for the benefit of the occupiers of common land. The Award was written in French and was signed on 1 May 1360.[1] The provisions bound all future Lords of Epworth Manor to permit certain benefits in perpetuity. The specific items were:

1. The said Lord of the Manor shall not approve any waste, moors, woods, or make any other APPROVEMENTS in the Isle of Axholme.
2. The said tenants, their heirs and assigns, shall have their common, appendant to their free tenements, as they have been used, time out of mind.
3. They may dig in moors and marshes, turfs, trees and roots found in the soil.
4. One pound, half an acre in size, shall be made at their cost and maintained by the Lord and his heirs in Belton Carr and another of the same size in Haxey Carr. Beasts to be impounded only once a year.
5. In the unenclosed parts, beasts shall not be impounded but driven out. Tenants may dig turf for house walls, and make tiles for roofs etc. and bring trees to repair the banks of the Trent.
6. Tenants shall not hereafter be fined for not appearing to ring their swine.
7. They may put hemp to be rated [retted] in all the waters of the island, except the skiers reserved to the Lord.[2]
8. The Lord shall not molest their dogs.
9. The tenants may fish in all the waters of the island except the aforesaid reserved skiers, and may dig turfs and other earths to improve their land.
10. Such tenants as are bound to enclose the Lord's lands may take underwood for hedges.

These were far reaching concessions though they included some obligations upon the tenants, such as repairing the Trent banks.

The troubled relationships between the Mowbrays and the Crown were resumed after John's death on the battlefield before

Constantinople. His son, Thomas, who became the first Earl Marshal of England, was eventually banished into exile for treachery. His son, despite his tender years (he was only 14 when his father died) became involved in revolt and was beheaded at York by Richard II in 1405. Despite these vicissitudes the Award remained in force as a bulwark for the local peasantry. This applied equally when the Manor of Epworth passed to Thomas Stanley, Earl of Derby, during the reign of Henry VII. By a further exchange the estate reverted to the Crown in the reign of Elizabeth I.

In the Middle Ages major works of drainage improvement and flood protection were undertaken only when needs became desperate.[3] The procedure usually involved setting up a commission which was given statutory powers to recruit manpower and procure equipment. This process had its origins long before in the drainage of Romney Marsh. In addition to such commissions or Courts of Sewers, monastic bodies undertook remedial work. With wide interests and adequate finances they carried out some important schemes both in the Isle of Axholme and in other fenland districts. The religious house of Newburgh, founded by the Mowbrays, was responsible for the construction of a landing stage at Owston Ferry. The cost of installation and upkeep was met by tithes from Owston parish and these were handed down in later years to the Archbishop of York.

In 1413 Geoffrey Gaddesby, formerly Abbot of Selby, constructed a sluice on Mardyke, near the village of Luddington.[4] The sluice controlled the Adlingfleet Don to the Trent. Gaddesby's motives in this work were stated to have been purely altruistic, though the Abbey lands must have benefited.

Notes

1. Peck, W. (1813/14), op. cit.; Stovin, G., 'A brief Account of the Drainage of the Levels of Hatfield Chace and Parts Adjacent', MSS (1752); and Korthals-Altes, J. (1925), op. cit.
2. Skiers: apparently a purely local term for meres or shallow lakes. The etymology is obscure.
3. It is not known when such works as raising the main river banks were first undertaken.
4. Dunston, G. (1909), op. cit.

7 The Local Scene prior to the Drainage

By the early 1600s the inhabitants of the Hatfield-Axholme district had become well adapted to the mixed upland and fen environment. There was an increase in population, and the production of food and raw materials was yielding a reasonable degree of wealth and comfort.

The great Chace of Hatfield was the largest deer park in England, reputedly extending to 72,850 ha (180,000 acres).[1] It had long been royal property and within its boundaries forest law prevailed. The area included meres and marshland to the extent of about half its size.

The central hunting area was termed 'soft land', but 'hard land' outside could be entered by keepers to retrieve game. Hunting also took place north and east of Hatfield Chace in districts termed 'purlieus', in which forest law did not apply. Selby Abbey maintained a strong interest in these areas.

The density of the deer population in the Chace is difficult to ascertain. Figures quoted by writers vary considerably but the concentration was not large over such a wide area.[2] It was perhaps about one deer per 25 ha (62 acres), not dense by Scottish standards. Both red and fallow deer were present, though the fallow were said to have been confined to Conisbrough Park.[3] The Chace was disparked in 1629, the deer being transported to other parks. The clearance was not complete as it is recorded that a certain John Scandaren was paid £100 for bringing 40 red deer alive from Hatfield Chace to stock Burley Park, Oakham, on 30 December 1634.[4]

The governing hierarchy of the Chace was originally headed by the King's Bow Bearer.[5] Later this title seems to have become Surveyor General. The ranks, in declining order, were as follows: Master or Chief Forester, 5 Keepers (for the wards of Wroot, Hatfield, Broadholme, Clownes and Wrangles) and 25 Regarders, who controlled the bounds of the forest and who attended the forest Court. The revenues accruing to the Crown were low.[6] Rents from Hatfield, Thorne, Fishlake and Stainforth were quoted at £180 per annum in 1487-9 and as only £165 in 1607-8. Major hunts appear to have been fairly infrequent. There is reference to one in 1541, during the reign of Henry VIII, when 200 stags and does were killed in a single day. Corruption and extortion were rife and, hardly surprising for an unenclosed Chace, poaching was common. Those offenders who were caught were liable to be gaoled in Thorne Castle. The deer, on the other hand, were responsible for much crop damage on neighbouring farmland. The Chace was not completely forested, since Thorne and Hatfield Moors were peat covered and carrying only scrub, while there were extensive meres including Thorne, Messic and Tudworth. A considerable area of land was covered by water in winter, affording plentiful supplies of water fowl.

The region was based on an agricultural economy which incorporated hunting and fishing. Furthermore the agriculture was mainly pastoral. The peat fens were grazed and for each village it was usual for such summer grazing to be unstinted. Stock was often brought into the area from other districts. Crowle common provided such facilities and a charge was made, the grazing being controlled by four grass-men. Many grasslands were flooded from November to May and during this time alluvium ('natural warp') was deposited, improving the fertility. Dykes, bridges and fences were normally well maintained. In winter stock was kept on the higher land and was housed or yarded. Epworth and Westwood Manors are said to have kept 12,000 cattle during the cold months. Meanwhile the flooded fenland provided excellent opportunities for fishing and fowling. In Epworth Manor the local population was permitted to catch white fish on Wednesdays and Fridays. The main livestock included cattle, sheep and horses, in that order of importance. The cattle were used for beef production, for dairying and for draught purposes. Milk was mainly processed into butter and cheese. Hides and tallow were also marketed as by-products. Sheep were kept on most farms and the main product was a fairly poor quality wool. Horses were bred for home use and also for exporting to upland areas.

Arable crops occupied a relatively small proportion of the farm land except on the mineral soils of the islands.[7] Many modern farms retain features of the open fields in the Isle of Axholme (see Chapter 22). Barley was the most important crop, a large proportion being used in brewing. Beans and peas were grown extensively both for human and animal consumption. Wheat was grown but most of the bread was made from rye and barley. Hemp and later flax represented industrial raw materials produced in the region. Later, in the 19th century, a sack and canvas industry developed in the Isle of Axholme. Oats, however, do not appear to have been popular in the area. Coleseed and rape are not referred to in pre-Drainage records and the inference is that the Dutch may have been responsible for their introduction.[8] In 1646 Sir John Maynard in a political paper states: 'What is coleseed and rape, they are but Dutch commodities and but trash and trumpery'.

Peat was produced from the turbaries, mainly on common land. The exploitation of the Thorne and Hatfield material was to await the 19th century. Not only was the turbary peat used as fuel by the local population but there was a thriving export to the cities of Leeds and York. It was transported in the long thin boats of the local people to Turnbridge, near the junction of the old Don (north fork) and the river Aire where the turves were transferred to the Aire barges.[9]

Turnbridge developed a position of importance where the east-west road from Snaith and East Cowick to Rawcliffe crossed the Don. It was on the route of river traffic passing to and from the centre of Hatfield Chace before the Drainage and thus had strategic importance. There was a harbour where so-called 'squatters' from the Levels of the Chace brought their cargoes. A once prosperous inn in the settlement later became a farmhouse.

Turnbridge was still a town of some importance during the Civil Wars as the Parliamentarian forces used a depot there as a munitions store. In a foray from Pontefract Castle during its siege the Royalists succeeded in blowing up the explosives.

At this time farms in the Hatfield-Axholme area were mainly in the 0.5-2 ha (1-5 acre) size group. A farm of 8 ha (20 acres) was a large business. The division of some of the land was derived from the ancient gavelkind custom, by which the land was divided equally among the sons upon inheritance.[10] The land fertility of the upland and the drier parts of the fenland appears to have been quite high. Black sandy land in the parishes of Epworth, Haxey and Owston was worth £2 per ha (80p per acre) while the stiff Mercia Mudstone soil of the Isle was valued at £1.50 per ha (60p per acre) in terms of rental value. The richer soils could be cropped without fallowing, but in Crowle and Eastoft a fallow every fourth year was more common.

Dr Joan Thirsk alludes to the fact that prior to the Drainage the pressure of an increasing population was being felt on the farms.[11] More stock was kept and pasturage was often found to be running short. This was felt particularly on the commons, and inter-parish disputes over stints were developing.

Thus the picture of Hatfield and Axholme before 1626 is fairly clear. It was a reasonably balanced economy, making good use of upland and marshland. It was dependent on grazing livestock and especially on common pastures. The commons, even then, were under pressure from an expanding economy and population. The dramatic effect of the Drainage, which created arable land at the expense of commons and grassland, was to strike at the heart of the way of life throughout the region.

Notes

1. Tomlinson, J. (1882), op. cit.
2. Whitehead, G.K., *The Deer of Great Britain and Ireland* (Routledge and Kegan Paul, 1964).
3. Conisbrough Park: the village is situated some 7 km south-west of Doncaster and close to the River Don. The ruins of a Norman castle are preserved.
4. Whitehead, G.K. (1964), op. cit.
5. Wainwright, J., *History of the Wapentake of Strafford and Tickhill* (1826).
6. Metcalfe, B. (1960), op. cit.
7. Thirsk, J., 'The Isle of Axholme before Vermuyden', *Agricultural History Review*, 1 (1953).
8. Coleseed (see also Chapter 22): the name derives from colza, a valuable source of lamp oil until the introduction of mineral oils. Rape is a variant of the same species (*Brassica napus L.*) and was developed as a fodder crop. Colza oil had long been used in England and there is a record of the streets of Wisbech in Cambrideshire being lit by this means in 1588. The coleseed

could have been grown locally, though equally it could have been an import from the Low Countries. In the 1970s and 1980s the crop known as oilseed rape (a recently selected variety of *B. napus*) has been widely grown, but the end-product is now a cooking oil.

9. Tomlinson, J, (1882), op. cit.
10. Gavelkind: Old English *gafol*, tribute; possibly connected with *giefan*, to give. This was a tenure traditionally associated with Kent by which land descended from the father to all sons (or to all daughters if there were no sons) in equal proportions and not by primogeniture.
11. Thirsk, J., *English Peasant Farming* (1957).

8 Royal Interest Leading to the Charles I Contract

During the reign of Queen Elizabeth I, in 1570, a disastrous flood occurred in the English fens and also in the Hatfield and Axholme district. While details are lacking there is no doubt that a good deal of hardship was caused. Not for the first time the government was alerted to the effects, political and economic, of such a calamity. The urge both to control floods and to reclaim land gave rise to many suggestions and recommendations, and amongst the pundits was the Frenchman Latreille. In 1584 he wrote a memoir on the subject of the drainage of the English fens. The work undoubtedly received the attention of that shrewd, far-seeing monarch, Queen Elizabeth. In 1589 she sought and received the advice of the leading water engineer of the day, Humphrey Bradley, who, though of English extraction, was a native of Bergen-op-Zoom in The Netherlands. Bradley had achieved fame in many European countries, but especially in France, where he was accorded the title of 'Master of the Dykes of France'. We have no precise details of his advice to the Queen but it is known that when drainage proposals were put to the fenland landowners whose land would have been affected they were received with prejudice and hostility. Such objections could not be over-ridden even by a powerful monarch and no major works took place during her reign, although some minor improvements were carried out.

Fenland drainage remained a possibility, if in abeyance. In 1600 an act was passed which permitted the recovery of very extensive areas of marshes in the Isle of Ely and the counties of Cambridge, Huntingdon, Northampton, Lincoln, Norfolk, Suffolk, Sussex, Essex, Kent and Durham. Surprisingly, Yorkshire is omitted. After succeeding Elizabeth in 1603, James I took up the royal interest in the subject and the reclamation of Hatfield Chace was probably in his mind.

Then, in 1609, an event took place that, in its melodramatic way, heralded the drainage of the Chace. Prince Henry, James I's elder son, invited a Dutch engineer to a deer hunting party in Hatfield Chace, ostensibly for sport, but probably also to reconnoitre drainage prospects. The party was accompanied by the Royal Bow Bearer, Sir Robert Swift, and Sir Henry Lee of Edenthorpe, a village on the edge of the Chace. Arranged by Sir Henry with the help of a local squire, Robert Portington, the considerable party undertook a large scale deer hunt. Some 500 deer were rounded up and driven towards the hunting party who had embarked in over 100 boats on a local mere. According to some versions the lake concerned was Thorne Mere, but others refer to the smaller Tudworth Mere. Thither the deer were driven, the herd with their antlers presenting the appearance of a small floating wood. The water-borne hunters then moved into the herd, clubbing or spearing animals of their choice. This scene is portrayed in a contemporaneous painting by an unknown artist (see frontispiece). Prince Henry spent the night at Hatfield, thus completing the last recorded royal hunt in the Chace.

According to de la Pryme the Prince's Dutch guest was Cornelius Vermuyden, although it may well have been either Cornelius Liens or Cornelius Verneuil. Without doubt, however, the question of draining the area was discussed. Unfortunately for the possible promoters, Prince Henry, who was known for his enthusiasm, died while still young, in 1612. There was at this time an increasing ground-swell of opinion in favour of more and bigger drainage schemes at various locations, in particular in the southern fens (the Great Level) where many schemes were proposed and some carried out. Bills were introduced to Parliament in 1605 and 1607 to cover more extensive work, but these were not passed.

In 1606 James I had met the Dutch drainers Cornelius Liens and Cornelius Verneuil, who presented him with a scheme to drain the fens. Liens was a member of a famous family in Zeeland, connected with the Vermuydens and involved deeply in reclamation work. Although the first proposal was not adopted, further contact was made with James in 1618 by another member of the Liens family, Joachim. Ambassador Extraordinary at the Court of St James, Joachim Liens was host to an official Dutch delegation concerned with the North Sea herring fisheries. On this occasion land drainage was also discussed, perhaps with more enthusiasm. Though nothing concrete appears to have been achieved, Joachim Liens nevertheless left for home with an English knighthood!

From about this time the English drainage scene became dominated by the enigmatic personality of Cornelius Vermuyden.[1] H.C. Darby states: 'Over all the history of the fen undertaking lies the shadow of Vermuyden. He was generally unpopular and was disliked by his colleagues, yet the force of circumstances again and again thrust him to the front.'[2]

Born in the Zeeland village of Sint Maartensdijk on the former Island of Tholen in 1590, Cornelius was immersed in land reclamation from an early age. The family was descended from a Fleming, Colaird van der Muden, who came to Zeeland by reason of his drainage skills. He established himself in Tholen despite the disputes which then persisted between The Netherlands and Flanders.

Cornelius was the son of Gillis Vermuyden and Sara, née Werckendets. The families involved in reclaiming polders from the sea were close-knit and the Liens, Werckendets and Croppenburghs were intimately connected. Johan Vermuyden, who was a first cousin of Cornelius, lived at Kettingdyk, a nearby hamlet, in a house which, in the 1970s, still proudly displayed the inscription ' 't Huys Vermuyden'. Johan married his cousin, Suzanne Liens, daughter of the before-mentioned Joachim, and the wedding took place in London.

Thus a connection between Cornelius Vermuyden and the English Court had been made, and full advantage was taken by that most ambitious of men. It is believed that Vermuyden first worked in England in 1621. He was involved in repairs to the break in the Thames bank at Dagenham and was undoubtedly introduced by Cornelius Liens. Vermuyden was also concerned with constructing a sea wall around Canvey Island, in the lower Thames, working with his kinsman Joos Croppenburgh. James I then employed Vermuyden on drainage work in the Royal Park at Windsor. It is reported that James then asked him to submit a plan for draining the Cambridgeshire Fens, but no more is heard of this particular request.

When James died in 1625 his successor Charles I maintained the royal enthusiasm, in spite of local doubts as to the possibility of draining Hatfield Chace. Within a year of his accession the King signed a contract with Cornelius Vermuyden for the drainage of the Chace and adjacent areas. Payment by the King would be in the form of land grants, with the reclaimed area to be divided equally between the Crown, Vermuyden and the commoners.

Vermuyden proceeded to the main Dutch money market in Amsterdam in order to raise funds for the work. Amsterdam was well accustomed to providing capital for such ventures in a number of countries. An *onderneming* (operating company) was assembled. There were eventually 57 members and in England they were termed 'Participants'. All except two of the company were Dutch or Flemish, the exceptions being Sir James Campbell and Sir John Ogle. Their adventure capital was to be secured against land allocations and since they had little means of assessing the potential development value of the land it must have been a highly speculative investment.

Notes

1. Harris, L.E., *Vermuyden and the Fens* (1953); and Korthals-Altes, J. (1925), op. cit.
2. Darby, H.C., *The Draining of the Fens* (Cambridge University Press, 1956).

9 The Dutchmen: Their Operations at Home and Abroad

At this point it would be useful to study the strong association of the Dutch with land drainage and, briefly, to see how this feature developed.[1]

Although land drainage and irrigation were practised by the Sumerians in 4000 BC and later by the Etruscans in Italy, developments in Northern Europe appear to have originated with the Frisians. This Teutonic tribe from southern Sweden moved into the Wadden Sea frontage of the Low Countries and North Germany, where they established themselves precariously on mounds or 'terpen' in the marshy areas. The terpen were constructed from surrounding soil to a height of between 4 and 10 m and they varied in area up to 5 ha. These self-contained units developed agriculturally and were also concerned with arts and crafts. It was probably the joining up of several terpen which gave rise to the concept of the sea wall by the 9th century. When such a wall was constructed to include a circle of terpen, the inside area could be protected from sea tides and flooding. This enclosure represented a polder in primitive form and with it developed the means of evacuating water and improving the wall construction. Thus the terpen were superseded and the way was open for extensive reclamation of land all along the shallow North Sea frontage.

Technical knowledge increased and spread to the Flemish people of the west where activity became intense from the 13th century. Monastic orders, in particular the Cistercians, and the landed nobility were prominent instigators of drainage work, and the name of Count William 'The Dyker' was to the fore. Between 1200 and 1500 some 300 ha per annum were reclaimed from sea and marsh, and by the mid-17th century this figure had reached 1,800 ha per annum.

Until the 15th century the only power available for pumping water was manpower or horsepower. The deep excavation of peat for fuel resulted in great problems when such areas became flooded. The windmill was invented in the southern Netherlands to provide greater power for lifting water. Though the maximum lift was originally only 1.5 m the windmill was a revolutionary development in inland drainage. Later improved designs doubled the lift, and by using a train of mills (*molengang*) water could be raised from much greater depths. The windmill's fame spread fast and a thriving export trade developed. Most of the earliest mills in England arrived in 'knocked-down' packaging for local erection. The great Dutch engineer Leeghwater (1575-1650) was especially associated with the use of windmills. One of his greatest achievements was the drainage of Lake Beemster in 1612 when he reclaimed nearly 7,000 ha by employing 43 windmills.[2]

The question may be asked as to why no windmills were employed in Hatfield Chace. The subject will be touched upon later but it is probable that no great depths of water were involved and that Vermuyden concerned himself with utilising and improving river flows.

The bucket dredger, consisting of buckets on a chain driven by wooden gearing, was invented in The Netherlands at about the same time as the windmill, and this machine was probably used by Vermuyden.

The 17th century was the Golden Age for the Dutch whose reputation spread far and wide. Their advice was sought by many countries and experts such as Leeghwater, Verlingh and Bradley were much in demand (Table 3).

Skilled workers were available to accompany foreign projects. One such group known as the 'Polderjongen' ('Polder Boys') came from the Biesbosch-Dordrecht district. With such a monopoly of talent it is not surprising that the Dutch were a *sine qua non* for the work at Hatfield Chace.

Table 3 Some early drainage works by Dutch engineers outside The Netherlands

Date	Location of drainage works
1100	Eiderstedt (by Frisian settlers)
1130	Wilster Marsh, Hamburg (by Frisians and men of Utrecht)
1140-64	Elbe marshes
1297	Prussian Netherlands (now Poland)
1515	Amager Island, Copenhagen
1555-1634	Dutch settlements in Schleswig-Holstein
1600-1700	Brandenburg Peat Bog, Berlin
1618	Göteborg Marsh, Sweden
1500-1825	Poland, extensive works
1599-1690	France, many projects, especially in Charente-Gironde districts
1621-1650	England
1622-1707	Italy, Pontine marshes
1700	Tilsit
1792	United States, Erie Canal
1788-1859	Russia

Notes

1. Wagret, P., *Polderlands* (Methuen, 1968); Smith, C.T., *Historical Geography of Western Europe before 1800* (Longman, 1978).
2. Lake Beemster was located some 25 km north of Amsterdam, in North Holland.

10 The Drainage Operation

The articles of agreement between Charles I and Cornelius Vermuyden to drain Hatfield Chace are dated 24 May 1626.[1] The lands concerned were Hatfield Chace and Ditch Marsh (now Dikes Marsh), the manors and lordships of Wroot and Finningley and of the Isle of Axholme, and 'Divers other lands'. These included lands on each side of the Idle, abutting on Dunn (the Don) and Ayre (the Aire) and Trent to the south and, somewhat unexpectedly, the manor of East Greenwich in London.[2] The total area was given as 60,000 acres (24,280 ha).

The provisions were specific, prescribing:

a) that Charles 'having regard as well to his own benefit as the good and welfare of his subjects inhabiting near or about the places aforesaid is desirous that the said drowned and surrounded grounds ... may be laid dry and made useful';
b) that Cornelius Vermuyden 'make same fit for tillage or pasture ... and shall forever maintain fit for tillage or pasture';
c) that a start to the work be made within three months by which time all claims and grants were to be dealt with from various persons;
d) that Cornelius Vermuyden, 'His heirs and assigns', or his nominees and their heirs and assigns, receive one third of the lands referred to;
e) that, in relation to the washes, Cornelius Vermuyden leave 'some small parcels of land on each or either side of the said several rivers for receptacles of the sudden downfalls of waters' (such lands were not to exceed 3,000 acres (1,214 ha) or 5 per cent of the whole area);
f) that Cornelius Vermuyden get full access to the land, secure materials and use existing watercourses and alter as necessary, with arrangements for compensation to be fixed by assessors;
g) that, on completion of the works, a corporation to ensure maintenance be appointed following nominations by Vermuyden;
h) that three years later six commissioners be appointed, three by the Lord Treasurer and three by Cornelius Vermuyden, with the remit

of viewing the works and estimating the yearly maintenance costs (land, which was unspecified, was to be conveyed to the six commissioners and the rents were to be used to cover maintenance costs); and

i) that all materials and men be admitted to the country free of customs and other impediment.

The obligation upon Vermuyden, and hence on the Participants jointly, to 'forever maintain [the land] fit for tillage or pasture' was a formidable undertaking. In the stormy days following the reclamation and at all subsequent times the commitment has remained binding; it is shouldered today by the great Water Authorities of Yorkshire and of Severn-Trent.

The requirement in the agreement to provide washes is notable. In the event these areas were wholly inadequate for the many floodings which occurred. Perhaps benefiting from the bitter experience of Hatfield, Vermuyden made massive provisions for reservoir areas in the Bedford Level years later. The setting up of a corporation was not finally secured until 1862.

The starting date prescribed in the agreement appears to have been observed with precision. As headquarters, depot and main operating base Vermuyden chose Sandtoft, at that time an island in the old River Idle. From the mid-12th century this place had been owned by St Mary's Abbey of York, although there is no record of a religious building. Sandtoft was also the site of some 200 houses for the workers who included Dutch, French, Flemish and Walloons. According to some accounts the frames for the houses were brought from The Netherlands, as were windmills, though the latter were used only for corn or oilseed milling. The population of Sandtoft reached about 1,000 by 1645 and the fact that it was an island made it a defensible site. Some type of fortification seems to have been erected during the troubled times, this being described by de la Pryme as 'Fort Dunkirk'. As Sandtoft was connected by river to the Aire and the Humber, material and workers could be transported by water from The Netherlands.

The approximate position of the watercourses in the Hatfield-Axholme basin which confronted Vermuyden at the outset of the project are shown in Figure 5. The main outfall rivers Ouse and Trent are tidal for considerable lengths, with banks which still form a rim well above the level of the central area. This rim must be pierced and controlled to provide exits for drainage channels. Such channels would therefore be unable to discharge at near high tide levels, and, since gravitation only was employed, their effectiveness was limited. Therefore Vermuyden's plan was first to intercept the main rivers entering the basin and lead them to points where continuous discharge was reasonably assured. The River Idle entering from the south was diverted by Vermuyden at the point known as Idle Stop (see aerial photograph on p. 12). Although there is some difference of opinion on the matter, it is highly probable that Vermuyden utilised the ancient Bykersdyke to convey the Idle water to the Trent at West Stockwith. The Dutch engineer probably straightened the alignment, deepened the channel and raised the banks. It appears that at first there was no sluice to prevent tidal ingress. However, in 1629, the Court of Sewers compelled John Liens, a Dutch Participant, to erect a sluice at Misterton Soss to improve conditions on Misterton and Haxey Commons.[3]

At the northern extremity of the Chace Vermuyden embanked the north arm of the Don and, enlarging the channel, blocked the easterly arm so that the whole of the flow of this river passed into the Aire below Turnbridge. Later the Adlingfleet branch of the Don was discontinued north of Dirtness. A barrier bank, known as the Ashfield Bank, was constructed on the south bank of the Don near the present town of Stainforth. This bank was of considerable size and remains of it can still be detected. According to Metcalfe it was 6 miles (10 km) long and extended to Turnbridge.[4] Most old maps do not indicate its extension northwards. However, banks certainly protected the Participants' land in Dikes Marsh and these would correspond with the Thorne-Turnbridge road (A 614T) which is on raised ground on the side of the Don. As outlined in Chapter 3, there is now very strong evidence to show that the lower Don was an artificial channel. Thus the banks would probably have been already high before the Drainage.

The smaller river Torne and the central marshy area remained to be dealt with. As an outfall for the collected waters of this complex Vermuyden chose Althorpe on Trentside (Figure 5). To this point he

Figure 5 Hatfield and Axholme, before and after the Drainage

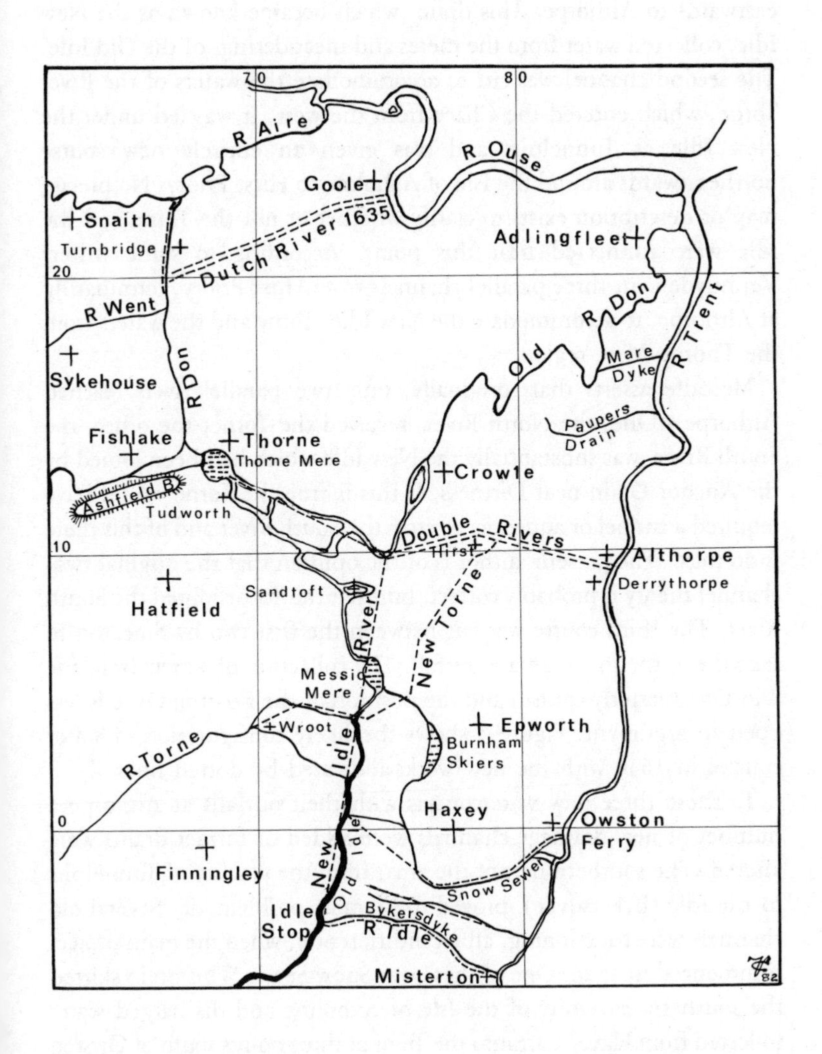

Principal Drainage Works

0 km 5

cut new watercourses each with its own discharge. The first was a drain commencing just below Idle Stop and running northwards for 13 km in a straight line to a central point at Dirtness. Thence it turned abruptly eastwards to Althorpe. This drain, which became known as the New Idle, collected water from the meres and meanderings of the Old Idle. The second channel was cut to accommodate the waters of the River Torne, which entered the Chace from the west. It was led under the New Idle at Tunnelpits and was given an entirely new course northeastwards around the Isle of Axholme to Hirst Priory. No precise map or description exists to clarify whether or not the Torne and the Idle were connected near this point. According to some writers Vermuyden cut three parallel channels from Hirst Priory, terminating at Althorpe, to accommodate the New Idle, Torne and the waters from the Thorne Mere region.

Metcalfe asserts that, originally, only two parallel rivers reached Althorpe.[5] One, the North River, received the Torne; the other, the South River, was substantially the New Idle which had been joined by the Anchor Drain near Dirtness. If this is true the Torne would have required a tunnel or aqueduct to cross the South River and of this there is no trace. The present author is of the opinion that the original two-channel theory is probably correct, but that the Torne joined the South River. The third course was cut between the first two by Smeaton to take the Torne to a separate outfall. The collection of waters from the Old Don (easterly course) and the position of the Boating Dyke is less open to argument. Figure 5 shows the likely configuration of water courses in 1630 with the new works indicated by dotted lines.

To these three new watercourses with their outfalls at Althorpe a number of new drainage channels were added or former drains were altered. The southern part of the area, from the vicinity of Tunnelpits to the Idle (Bykersdyke), proved to be most problematic. Several old channels were functioning, albeit indifferently, when the main project commenced in 1626. One of these was Snow Sewer. This drain skirted the southern extremity of the Isle of Axholme and discharged water collected from Haxey Carr into the Trent at three points south of Owston Ferry. The three forks comprised Snow Sewer proper (apparently the widest channel), Queen's New or Middle Sewer, and Queen's Old Sewer or King's Old Sewer. It appears that Vermuyden deepened and straightened the western end of Snow Sewer, connecting it to a drain which had been constructed parallel to, and east of, the New Idle. He may have installed sluices at the main discharge, and almost certainly he blocked two of the old forks, though possibly at a later date. The Monkham Drain, originating near Epworth Carr, was cut by Vermuyden, apparently to improve Participants' land in that area. Originally, Monkham's Drain probably connected with Snow Sewer, possibly near Langholme. Later, however, the drain had an independent discharge channel closely parallel to Snow Sewer. Today the course is known as Ferry Drain.

Between Snow Sewer and the main Idle (Bykersdyke) an ancient ditch, Heckdyke, was probably improved by the Participants as the land on each side was reclaimed and allocated.[6] The line of this ditch forms part of the Nottinghamshire-Humberside county boundary. Land between it and Bykersdyke was formerly owned by the Duchy of Lancaster.

No details are available of the methods of surveying, excavation, transport of material and co-ordination employed in this complex operation. Doubtless all the techniques known to the Dutch and Flemish engineers would have been applied. However, it is probable that the Hatfield and Axholme conditions would have had no exact parallel in the previous experiences of Vermuyden and his associates. This can be fairly safely surmised from the shortcomings which were revealed. Nevertheless, the undertaking was faced with extremely small gradients, varied soils and difficult tidal restrictions at the outfalls. The operation was not one of creating a polder, from which water would need to have been lifted. Hence, no windmills were employed for pumping. The flows of rivers and dykes to the tidal outfalls were relied upon even though the actual freeboard at the discharge point was small and of limited duration. It is probable that scoop-wheels operated by horses or men were used to clear small flooded areas of water. To add to the technical problems Vermuyden had to counter sullen or active hostility on the part of the local inhabitants whose resentment was almost total.

It is therefore remarkable that the completion of the entire operation was declared by Vermuyden within 18 months of its commencement. There were no precedents for such an operation, which, even by modern standards, would have been a staggering achievement. The boldness and courage of the promoters stand out in spite of the subsequent aftermath of strife and disappointments. However, it is quite clear that the work was far from finished even by 1633. The pressures to speed the work were intense. The Drainage had been financed by funds raised mainly in The Netherlands, and the Participants could only commence to pay for their loans by bringing their land awards into production. The speculative element was strong at all times and there is good reason to suppose that the lands first 'reclaimed' had been of good initial potential. In the hearings of a special suit brought by the 'Gentlemen of Epworth' against the Participants in 1685 interesting evidence was supplied by aged witnesses.[7] One, aged 78, claimed that drainage work had not improved local land. Some 3,000 ha acquired by Vermuyden had been the best land before drainage, being worth three times the value of land elsewhere. Witnesses spoke of 'pretended drainage', suggesting that the Participants had taken advantage of the Hatfield Chace Agreement to secure the best land.

The Participants lost no time in claiming their land and it was parcelled and allocated, while the active owners sought local residences. Of the 60,000 acres (24,280 ha) a third was awarded to Cornelius Vermuyden, his heirs and assigns, which embraced all the Participants. A third became Crown property and the final third was virtually handed back to the Commoners. The cost of the work up to this point had been £175,000. Almost immediately transfers and sales of land commenced, and these changes were to become a feature of the area for many years to come. In 1629 Vermuyden purchased from the King, Hatfield Manor, Brampton, Hatfield Park, Fishlake, Thorne, Stainforth, Dowsthorpe (Sykehouse), and a number of smaller holdings, all for the sum of £10,000 and a ground rent of £150 per annum.[8] In addition half of the 2,600 acres (1,052 ha) of Misson Waters and Commons were conveyed for their lives to Cornelius Vermuyden and his daughters Sarah and Catherine for £180 per annum ground rent. The Crown had already contributed £10,000 to cover drainage works in the Misson area.

Some idea of the distribution of the reclaimed land amongst the Participants is provided by the map prepared by Josias Arelebout in 1639.[9] The map shows the parcels of land taken up by the following:

Figure 6 Lands of the Participants, 1639

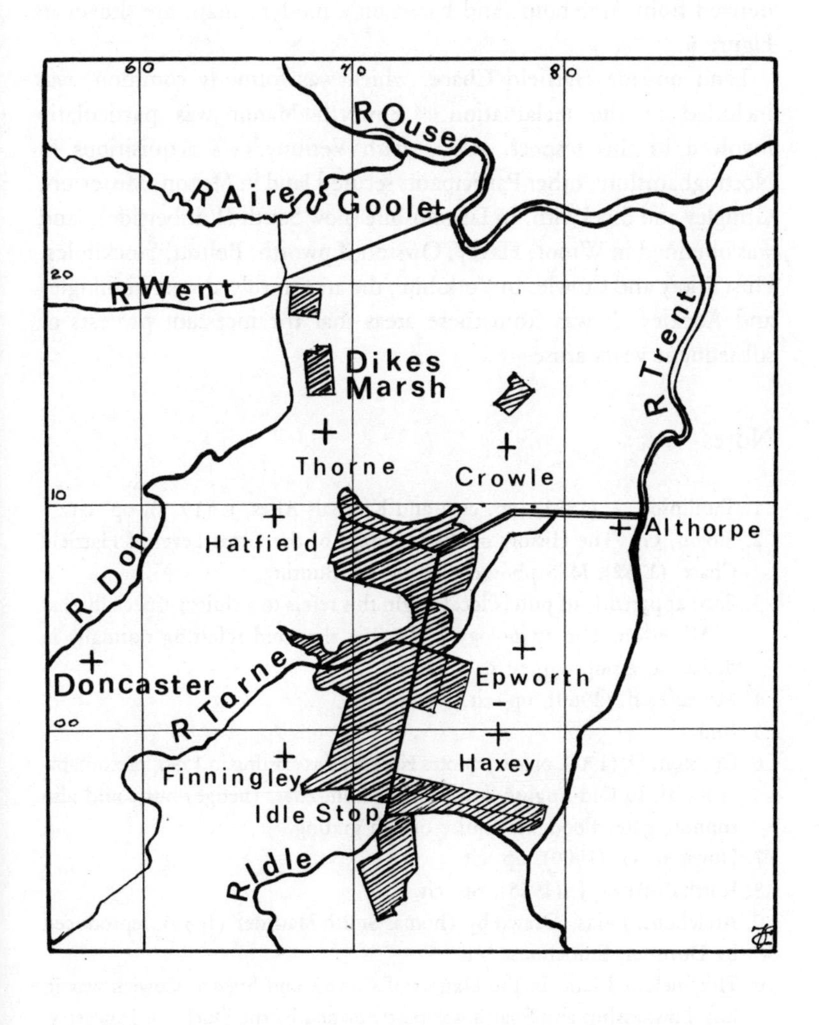

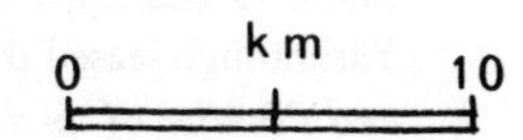

Source: Josias Arelebout (1639), adapted

Sir Philip Vernatti, Cavell (*cum suis*), Cornelius Vermuyden, Gaell of Dordrecht, Mr Valkenburgh, Mr Corselis and Mr Borchard. The list and the land described are not complete, but the approximate locations, derived from Arelebout, and based on a modern map, are shown in Figure 6.

Land outside Hatfield Chace, which was formerly common, was included in the reclamation.[10] Epworth Manor was particularly involved in this respect. Along with Vermuyden's acquisitions in Nottinghamshire, other Participants secured land in Misson, Misterton, Gringley and Stockwith. In Lincolnshire (now South Humberside), land was obtained in Wroot, Haxey, Owston, Epworth, Belton, Stockholes, Hirst Priory and Crowle. In Yorkshire, the areas involved were Finningley and Auckley. It was from these areas that the incessant protests of subsequent years arose.

Notes

1. Tomlinson, J. (1882), op. cit.; and Korthals-Altes, J. (1925), op. cit.
2. Stovin, G., 'The History of the Drainage of the Great Level of Hatfield Chace' (1752), MSS photocopied by W. Bunting.
3. Soss: apparently of purely local origin this refers to a sluice, especially that of Misterton. The etymology is obscure, the word referring normally in dialect to a sloppy mess or mixture.
4. Metcalfe, B. (1960), op. cit.
5. Ibid.
6. Dunston, G. (1909, op cit.) quotes Heckdyke as existing in 1596, presumably artificial. In Old English *heck* derives from *haecc* (hedge) but could also connote gate, floodgate, sluice or fish grating.
7. Dunston, G. (1909), op. cit.
8. Korthals-Altes, J. (1925), op. cit.
9. Arelebout, Josias, 'Drawn by Thomas Smith Marriner' (1639), reproduced by Dunstan, Stonehouse, etc.
10. This included land in the Manors of Cowick and Snaith. Cowick was in Royal ownership and Snaith was partly owned by the Duchy of Lancaster. These estates appear to have reverted to the Crown and Sir Thomas Yarborough leased them in 1730-1 (Robinson, C.B., *History of the Priory and Peculiar of Snaith* (1861)).

11 The Participants and their Workers

The personal stories both of the Participants and of their workers would justify individual accounts if more were known of them. Unfortunately details are available of only a few of the many aliens who braved a hostile reception in 17th-century England. An attempt was made by John Hamilton to cover the history of the period in two romantic novels, *The Manuscript in a Red Box* and *Captain John Lister*, stories whose fictional characters include foreign drainers and local inhabitants. They form interesting reconstructions of some of the events in the Axholme area as they might have occurred.[1]

There were 57 Participants but it would appear that not all took up active land occupation. The list in Table 4 is derived from Stovin, Stonehouse and others.[2] The spellings vary between accounts. The total area is in excess of the Contract award but it probably includes land purchased from the Crown by Vermuyden immediately after the formal

Table 4 The Participants and land owned by them

Name	Hectares (approximate)	Acres
* van Baerle, Johann *et al.* (Amsterdam)	405	1,000
van Beueren (*or* Beveren), Cornelius (Dordrecht)	526	1,300
* van Beueren (*or* Beveren), Abraham	?	
* Bocard (*or* Boccaert), Andrew (land shared with J. Corsellis)		
Bushop, Edward, widow of	162	400
de Bruxelles, Charles (Dordrecht)	40	100
Campbell, Sir James (British)	243	600
Cats, Sir James (Dordrecht)	27	67

* Cats, Leonard (Middleburg)	81	200
Cornolison, Reijnier	40	100
Corsellis, John (land shared with A. Bocard)	1,457	3,600
Craijosteijn, Michael (Dordrecht)	81	200
* Cruyspenninck (*or* Crupenincke), Pieter (Amsterdam)	178	440
* van Darin (*or* Dueren), Marcellus	162	400
Dolens, Abram	81	200
Droogboot, Jacob (heirs of) (Middleburg)	32	80
Franken, Roolof and Sebastian (Dordrecht)	81	200
de Gelder, Wouter (Dordrecht)	40	100
Goel, the Professor	40	100
* Hinloopen, Tymon Jacobs	?	
Jacobson, Philip	142	350
* Kingsten, John	?	
* Lyens (*or* Liens), John	?	
Ogle, Sir John (British)	137	339
van Peenin, Isaac and Pieter	231	572
van Peenin, Samuel	477	1,178
Somoij, Derrick (heirs of) (Amsterdam)	121	300
Struys, Abram (Dordrecht)	101	250
Struys, Jacob	61	150
* van Valkenburgh, Lucas	505	1,247
* van Valkenburgh, Marcus	464	1,146
* van Valkenburgh, Sir Matthew	328	811
Vandace (*or* Vandael), Dionysius, widow of	65	160
Vandimen, John	40	100
Vermuyden, Sir Cornelius	1,843	4,554
* Vernatti, Abram	222	550
* Verbatti, Sir Philibert	1,275	3,150
* Vliet, Fabian (The Hague)	81	200
Vos, Regnier Cornelisen (Dordrecht)	40	100
* de Vries, Dingman	?	
* van Weely, William (Amsterdam)	146	361
* de Witte, Jacob	?	
Total	9,957	24,605

completion of the Drainage. Normally aliens would not have been permitted to own English land, but a special Grant of Denization was made by Charles I in 1629 in favour of a number of the Participants, whose names are marked in Table 4 by an asterisk.[3]

It can be seen from Table 4 that Cornelius Vermuyden, who was knighted on completing the Drainage, dominated the new landowners with his acquisition of almost 1,850 ha of land. He built a house in the Dutch style at Crowtrees Hall, close to Sandtoft, although he is said to have lived at one time in Thorne.[4] The Crowtrees house was at first of timber but it was later reconstructed in brick and tile.

The van Valkenburgh family received a large area of reclaimed land but, as in the case of many Participants, they failed to establish themselves permanently. Sir Matthew had built a house at Middle Ings, on the Idle, where he died in 1644. His widow, Dame Isabella, followed him in the same year and their two sons later returned permanently to The Netherlands. One of Sir Matthew's brothers died at Crowle 'in very low circumstances' in 1653, having sold all his 800 ha of land.

Sir James Cats, famous in The Netherlands as a poet, statesman and speculator, was an original Participant, acquiring the Manor of Finningley, where he lived for a time.[5] This distinguished Dutchman was born at Brouwershaven in Zeeland in 1577. He became associated with the Universities of Leyden, Orléans and Paris. He was a Doctor of Law in Middleburg and then became Chancellor of the city of Dordrecht, an important centre for drainage financing. Cats made a fortune as partner in the drainage of the Groede Wateringue in The Netherlands. He married Susanna van Valkenburgh, sister of Lucas, Matthew and Marcus, thus completing family ties with the Drainage group. Sir James returned to The Netherlands and died in 1660 at Zorgvlied. Much less is known of the other Participants but in the aftermath of the Drainage the experiences of those who came to the Chace were unhappy to the point of proving disastrous.

Many were unable to repay their loans or even to meet drainage 'scots' (rates).[6] Some defaulted in paying their workers' wages. Furthermore the period was marked by continuous lawsuits and bickerings. Farming operations were seldom successful and within a few years most of the Dutch adventurers had returned home, poorer, and embittered with their experiences.

If the Participants left little trace of their contributions their workers made a greater impact on the Chace. Their former presence is obvious from certain names which are still used today, such as Jaque's Cottage, Smaque Farm and Dutch River. A certain amount is known of these artisans and of their ill-fated Sandtoft settlement. Cornelius Vermuyden was assisted by specialist engineers from The Netherlands and he is said to have paid them £50 each per annum. One of his main Dutch assistants from the start of the work was David Prole, but nothing further is known of this man.[7] How valuable would have been his working diary! A certain John Noakes was the official bookkeeper and much later, in 1650, he was confirmed in this post by a Decree of the Court of Sewers. At the same time Prole was appointed surveyor, while Henry Cooke and Cyprian Vanderart were created overseers of works and assistants to Noakes. A certain Richard Carvile was appointed Bailiff. Stovin quotes the following names of certain 'officers and workmen': John Lemairs, Nicholas Donson, Christian Vanderart, Pieter Vangolder, Pieter Riddoe, Edward Lyons (or, more probably, Liens), John Debort and Robert Ginstrons.

Of the many foreign workers engaged in The Levels some had already been employed elsewhere in England. Dutch engineers had undertaken minor works, for example, Janszoon at Yarmouth, Frieston at Wells, van Croppenburg (helped by Vermuyden) at Canvey Island and Dagenham in Essex. Thus some experience in English conditions was available. The high proportion of French Protestant workers was associated with events in France at the time. During the period when Cardinal Richelieu was Prime Minister to King Louis XIII of France great pressure was exerted upon the Huguenots, despite the religious freedom they were granted under the Edict of Nantes in 1598. This influence culminated in the ultimate destruction of the Huguenot 'capital', La Rochelle, in 1629. Thus many of these talented, industrious people decided to leave France and to find openings for their skills in the England of Charles I. To the Hatfield-Axholme area they brought their knowledge of spinning, weaving, dyeing and tanning. It seems possible that the growing of colza or oilseed rape was introduced by the Dutch to England in the Hatfield Chace at this time.[8]

The work force was not quite exclusively foreign but local workers appear to have been attracted only in small numbers and at higher than usual wage rates. Later, when the construction of the New, or Dutch, River was undertaken, a rather higher proportion of English workers seems to have been employed. It has been suggested this may have been part of a policy to allay local criticism of excessive foreign participation.

In the contract between Charles I and Vermuyden provision was made for the erection of one or more chapels for the benefit of the workers housed at Sandtoft. Though there is reason to believe that this proposal at first encountered the opposition of Archbishop Laud, a church was eventually built, complete with a burial ground. It was to experience an eventful career in the troubled times which were to come. Worshippers were at first accommodated in the house of Pierre Smaque at Crowtrees and later in Philibert Vernatti's barn. They received the offices of Pastor Petrus Bontemps, apparently in a voluntary capacity. Then a certain Isaac Bedloe was prevailed upon to erect a Protestant Church on a Sandtoft site. No details of the structure have come to light but the unfortunate Mr Bedloe was never paid for the building and as a result suffered financial ruin.[9] Whether the church was faulty or whether the congregation was unable to raise funds is unknown. Arrangements were made to hold services in Dutch on Sunday mornings and in French in the afternoons. The first paid minister was a John (or Jean?) Despagne who died in 1655 and was buried at Crowle. There were six successive ministers, the last being a Mr Vanely. As will be mentioned later, the church was damaged by rioters in 1650, subsequently repaired but again attacked. By 1686 it was in ruins, and shortly afterwards no remains were visible. However, in recent times, cut stones from a building were dug up on a site in Sandtoft village and preserved by Mr G. Hurst of Epworth.[10] It is highly possible that these were from the settlers' church.[11] The church register was in existence until the 1920s, when it vanished mysteriously. Earlier writers such as Stovin quoted extensively from this record but the loss is a serious one when so few contemporaneous records exist.

Notes

1. Hamilton, J.A., *The Manuscript in a Red Box* (1903) (Bodley Head, Fair Books, 1966). An unpublished dramatised version of the story was produced by W.A. Ross of Belton. Hamilton, J.A., *Captain John Lister* (Hutchinson, 1906; reprinted by Scholar Press and Mechanics Institute, Epworth, 1978).
2. Stovin, G. (1752), op. cit.; and Stonehouse, W.B., *History and Topography of the Isle of Axholme* (1839; reprinted by Mechanics Institute, Epworth, LX32143).
3. Moens, W.J.C., *Proceedings of the Huguenot Society of London*, Part ii (1889), pp. 266-81.
4. Tomlinson, J. (1882), quoting a Mr Gossip, stated that Old Hall, Thorne, was Vermuyden's 'temporary home'.
5. Korthals-Altes, J. (1925), op. cit.
6. Scot: a payment similar to a rate or tax or assessed contribution. Origin: Middle English from Old Norse *skot*.
7. Stovin, G. (1752), op. cit.
8. Colza: see Chapter 7, note 8.
9. De la Pryme (1698) remembered the walls of the church standing in 1686-7. They were 'on the north side of the bank coming from Bearswood Green to New Idle Bank, near opposite Mr. Reading's last built house which stands on the south side of the said bank'. He also remembered the building (*sic*) and demolishing of Fort Dunkirk 'and have rode over ye grounds it was built on to defend it from ye Islanders before the land was enclosed'.
10. Anon., *Epworth and its Surroundings* (Barnes and Breeze and the *Epworth Bells, c.* 1904). In this booklet the Mission Church at the West End, Epworth, is mentioned. It was built by Canon Overton in 1886 and it incorporated a corner stone obtained from Sandtoft inscribed with the date 1686.
11. Loughlin, N. and Miller, K.R. (1980), op. cit. The authors state that the stones from the Sandtoft church were used locally for repairing roads. They confirm the above reference to the Mission Church and further state that the Sandtoft font was reportedly taken to Tetley Hall near Crowle (a former home of the Stovin family!)

12 Descendants of the Foreign Community

The best-known of the immigrants who joined Vermuyden in the Drainage was the de la Pryme family, who had owned substantial estates on the continent.[1] One branch had an estate at Paderborn, in Hesse-Kassel and another at Ypres in West Flanders, then part of France. The family became Protestant and a Charles de la Pryme emigrated to the Hatfield area in 1628, where he farmed. Presumably he bought land from one or other of the Participants but his operations were unrewarding and he incurred losses amounting to many hundreds of pounds. The family retained the Ypres estate but after the revocation of the Edict of Nantes in 1685, which curtailed the freedom of French Protestants, they were unable to recover their title. One of Charles's sons, Matthias, married a member of the Smaque family and their son was Abraham de la Pryme to whom we are indebted for the main account of the drainage of The Levels.

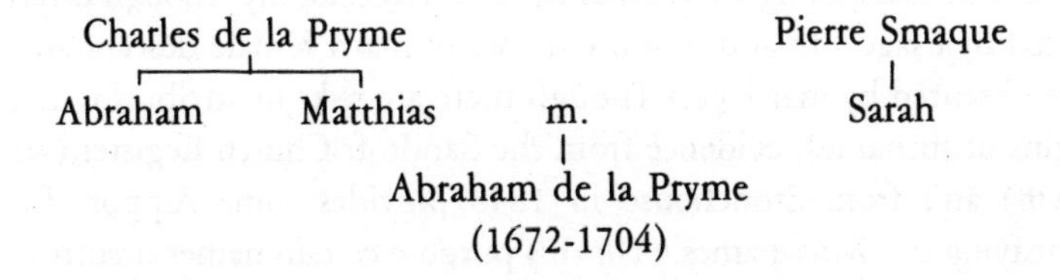

Educated at Cambridge where he graduated as a BA, the younger Abraham possessed considerable literary talent. He entered the church and became curate at Hatfield in 1696. During this period he concentrated on the history of Hatfield, this study culminating in *The History and Antiquities of the Town and Parish of Hatfield*. This work was contained in nine small manuscript volumes which were, unfortunately, never published. They are now in the British Museum (Lansdowne MSS 899). The only work by de la Pryme to be published was his diary, which has been used extensively by almost all subsequent historians.[2]

In 1698 de la Pryme left Hatfield for Kingston-upon-Hull where he was appointed curate and reader to the High Church.[3] There he pursued his interest in local history until 1701 when he left to become Vicar of Thorne. In that year he became a Fellow of the Royal Society, contributing papers to that body. He died in 1704. Although some authorities have questioned the accuracy of some of de la Pryme's statements, his work forms the most important source material for the area. There was, of course, no contemporaneous account of the Drainage; de la Pryme was writing some 70 years after the event.

The Smaque family is also of interest. Pierre Smaque, a wealthy Parisian Protestant, left France in 1630, apparently following political pressure. He took up residence at Crowtrees Hall in a large house said to have been built by one of the van Valkenburghs. The house must have been a large one, since services were held here prior to the construction of the Sandtoft chapel. Smaque Farm carries on the family name to this day. It is situated on the A 18 road near Dirtness bridge.

Although the colony of foreign workers which was established in the Chace remained stable for no more than 30 years, many families stayed in the vicinity of Yorkshire and Lincolnshire long afterwards. In a number of cases foreign surnames have survived locally, though often altered by usage.[4] In addition the names of many female descendants were obscured by marriage.[5] Though there are risks in attributing the origins of surnames, evidence from the Sandtoft Church Register (via Stovin) and from Stonehouse in 1838 provides some support for identifying surviving names.[6] For this purpose certain names occurring in current telephone directories for South Humberside/North Lincolnshire (1979) and Barnsley/Doncaster (1980) have been selected and arranged in Table 5.

Of particular interest are the names which survive from the original Church Register of Sandtoft. These were extracted by George Stovin, who had access to the document long before it was lost. The Huguenot names are very prominent and the Huguenot Society of London drew attention to them in 1889.[8]

The name of Dunderdale is frequent in the South Humberside/North

Lincolnshire district. Mentioned in old records, this English family name conceals a French ancestor, Peter (perhaps originally Pierre) le Leu. The presence of the Dutch name, Gelder, is interesting. There are no earlier references to it and there is some possibility that the name derived from a later Dutch 'invasion' when the Thorne Moor peat workings were developed in the 19th century.

A number of Dutch/French names, such as Le Plas, Descow and Tafinder, known to the Revd Stonehouse in 1838, have since disappeared.[9] Read, in 1858, records the names of Isle of Axholme freeholders who voted in the Parliamentary election of 1723. They contain no foreign names! He also gives a Directory, presumably for 1858, of principal landowners, occupiers, professionals and traders in the Isle. Names include Egarr, Cranidge, Brunyee and Taffinder (*sic*), but no others of obvious foreign ancestry. However, Jacques or Jaques is very much alive as a local name in our now predominantly urban society, as are Brunyee and Tyson.

For a considerable period after the Drainage the influence of the foreign workers was felt in the Hatfield Chace area. This was in spite of the hostility which existed, at least at first, between the immigrant and the native population. Writing in 1882, John Tomlinson noted: 'It is scarcely surprising that in and around Thorne should survive many evidences of Dutch occupation. The low single-pole wagon with "swingle bars" and chain traces is still in common use; which vehicle is adapted to the "Levels" but totally unsuitable for travelling up and down hills. Again, nowhere else but in this district have I seen cooked and partaken of "gofers" (from the Dutch word *gaufres*), a kind of trough-shaped cake made of batter and baked in an iron mould, which opens in the centre, resembling two "draught boards" with the squares indented. These "gofers" when toasted, well buttered and powdered with lump sugar are really a delicacy.'[10] John Wainwright, writing in 1826, went so far as to say: 'Indeed Thorne, Hatfield, Crowle, Wroot, Epworth, Haxey, Blaxton, Aukley and Finningley are half peopled by the posterity of Dutch and French settlers.'[11]

Clearly these immigrants have passed imperceptibly into the matrix of English society, leaving us today merely the tenuous link of names to remind us of their contributions.

Table 5 Surnames of former foreign workers and possible present-day counterparts

Name	Probable ethnic origin	Recorded on Sandtoft Church Register	Noted in 1839	Number of entries of present-day name in telephone directories: South Humberside/ North Lincolnshire		Barnsley/ Doncaster	
Amory	Dutch or French	x	x	Amery	6		0
Brunyee	Huguenot (Bryne)	x	x		2		9
Cranage[7]	Dutch				0	Cranidge	4
Dunderdale	English/ French descendant of Peter le Leu		x		14		2
Descow	Dutch or French		x		0		0
Delanoy	Huguenot	x		Delaney	3	Delany Delaney	7
Dumoulin	Huguenot	x		Dimoline	2	Dimaline	8
Egar	Dutch?	x	x	Egarr	9	Egarr Egar	2

Fontaine	Huguenot	x			3		0
Gelder	Dutch				9	Gelder	
						Geldard	37
						Geldart	
Harlay	Huguenot	x		Harley	2	Harley	16
Impson	Dutch or French	x		Empson (connection doubtful)	16	Empson	7
Jacques	French		x	Jacques	10	Jacques	26
				Jaques	18	Jaques	27
Le Plas	French or Walloon		x		0		0
Leroy	Huguenot,	x			2		0
Poree	Huguenot	x		Porri	1		0
Pryme	Huguenot	x		Priam	2		0
				Prime	5		
Rammery	Huguenot	x		Ramery	4		0
Renard	Huguenot	x		Renardson	2		0
Tafinder	Dutch		x		0		0
Tyssen or Tyson	Huguenot	x		Tyson	18	Tyson	10
Turgusin	Huguenot			Turgoose	8	Turgoose	9
				Turgoise	1		

Sources: Stovin (1752); Overend (Huguenot Society, 1889); and Stonehouse (1839)

Notes

1. Peck, W., (1813/14), op. cit.
2. De la Pryme, A. (*c.* 1698), op. cit.
3. High Church: the former name of the Holy Trinity Church of Kingston-upon-Hull, founded in 1285.
4. Le Moine, H.G.B., *Proceedings of the Huguenot Society of London*, Part ii (1889).
5. Names of female descendants: this refers to English-Settler marriages. The Dutch and French women tended to retain their surnames upon marriage with one of their own nationality.
6. Stovin, G. (1752), op. cit.; and Stonehouse, W.B. (1839), op. cit.
7. Cranidge: Le Moine (1889, op. cit.) mentions a certain J. Cranidge of Denaby as a descendant of a Dutch family of Sandtoft. He also states that Cranidge's ancestors brought silver from The Netherlands and melted it down. Two silver cups dated 1694 and 1700 were preserved. The treasure was first concealed at Crowtree in five casks.
8. Overend, G.H., 'The First 30 Years of the Foreign Settlement in Axholme (1626-1656)', *Proceedings of the Huguenot Society of London*, Part ii (1889).
9. Stonehouse, W.B. (1839), op. cit.
10. Tomlinson, J. (1882), op. cit.
11. Wainwright, J. (1826), op. cit.

13 The Immediate Aftermath of the Drainage

By 1629 it was already apparent that there were serious faults in the planning, calculation and execution of the works. Professor Lorentz, the great 20th-century Dutch scientist, spent eight years calculating the disturbances by currents and tides in the Zuyder Zee before reclamation was started. No such calculations preceded the Hatfield Chace project and the lack of realistic data must have contributed to the technical inaccuracies. In the first place the Don diversion into the Aire proved wholly unsatisfactory. Flooding was caused in Fishlake and Sykehouse, though the Participants' own land to the east and south of the northerly arm of the Don was protected by barrier banks. The town of Thorne also benefited from its position and was well served by the Ashfield barrier bank.

As a result of strong protests by the people of Fishlake and Sykehouse Vermuyden raised the left (west) bank of the Don but charged the complainants £200 per annum for the upkeep. In addition, nearer to Hatfield, commoners with rights over parts of Hatfield Chace wastes made strong representations to the Crown. This produced two sittings of the Lord President of the Council for the North which were held at Hatfield in 1630.[1] Thomas, Viscount Wentworth, Lord Darcy and Justice Hutton ruled that the ancient rights and privileges of the inhabitants of Hatfield Manor (the complainants) were to be restored and maintained, including the rights to dig turf and to fell timber. They were handed back 1,633 ha (4,035 acres) of land which would have been reclaimed and exploited by Vermuyden, who had bought the Manor from the King in 1629. This was a most serious blow to the leading Participant who withdrew from the jurisdiction of the Wentworth Court by conveying his land to trustees. Later, he was forced to dispose of all his interests and property, suffering considerable loss in the process. Nevertheless he remained a Participant and continued as 'Master of the Drainage'.

Vermuyden's purchaser for Hatfield Manor was John Gibbon (or Guibon). However, this action did not remedy the flooding experienced by the people living west of the lower Don and they continued to lodge their complaints. A further sitting of the Court took place and in the famous 'Wentworth Judgement' the Commission of Sewers demanded the construction of a new discharge point for the Don.[2] This was to take the form of a double channel cut eastwards from near Turnbridge to meet the Yorkshire Ouse at Goole. The ruling was confirmed by Order in Council in April 1633 with Wentworth ordering that all the Participants were to be assessed for the cost of the construction. This unexpected and huge financial obligation had a dramatic effect on the unity of the Participants. It was on the petition of his fellow adventurers that Vermuyden's property, or such of it as had not already been 'alienated', was placed in the hands of official receivers.[3] A series of legal actions ensued involving Vernatti, van Peen, van Valkenburgh and Corselis, while Vermuyden himself withdrew from the forefront of the Hatfield-Axholme scene.

The cutting of the New River, later to be known as Dutch River, was pushed forward. It is said that relatively highly paid local labour was employed in the work. The double channels became a single river as the fortuitous result of a severe flood caused by a sudden thaw some years later. The river became suitable for navigation providing access to the Doncaster and Sheffield areas. The Althorpe discharge soon showed its limited capacity, and it proved to be an unfortunate choice as the main outfall. It is difficult to understand Vermuyden's decision to use a point so far up the Trent when the very slight falls called for the lowest possible discharge point. The alignment of Idle Stop, Dirtness and Althorpe is in direct contrast to his later Bedford rivers, which, by their straight courses of 32 km provided maximum gradients and adequate scouring.

The third major shortcoming was the poor functioning of the New Torne. The Torne originally contributed to the meres and marshes of the central area and Vermuyden decided to construct a new channel around the north-western edge of the Isle of Axholme. This traversed fertile pasture land which had not previously been subject to flooding. The raised banks of the new river proved to be quite inadequate to contain the maximum flow and much damage resulted in times of flood. To this day the Torne remains a sensitive river despite improvements to pumping systems. The situation in the south of the area was not wholly satisfactory, especially north of the Idle (Bykersdyke). This district was liable to flooding from the main river and was to cause much trouble in future years.

Notes

1. Korthals-Altes, J. (1925), op. cit.
2. Stovin, G. (1752), op. cit.
3. Ibid.

14 Social Upheaval prior to the Civil Wars

If the technical problems created by the Drainage were serious they were dwarfed in their complexity by the social reactions. These were not helped by the rigid attitudes of the times, least of all by Vermuyden himself. In the words of John Tomlinson: 'Perhaps no great scheme like that of Vermuyden's could have been undertaken without disturbing immemorial rights, affecting the interests of a poor but widely scattered population and causing (at least for a time) distress and widespread disaffection. But the Dutch capitalist, secure of the King's favour and Court interest, appears to have prosecuted his work with a rigour approaching to injustice. In retaliation for widespread depredations he issued writs and subpoenas broadcast so that many neglecting to appear were cast into prison.'[1] A paper of 1701 also reflects the personal antipathy which Vermuyden attracted: 'A monster of a man whose natural qualities no one English epithet can answer'.[2]

The decision of Charles I to commence the drainage of the Chace in 1626 was a precipitate one. It was in keeping with the action of an absolute monarch to discount an ancient statute when this would have interfered with his personal ambition. The Axholme populace, however, was not cowed into submission. Although the commoners were awarded 8,000 ha (20,000 acres) in the Articles of Agreement of 1626 this was no substitute for the common rights granted to them in perpetuity by Lord Mowbray in 1360. The Articles had demanded that all claims and grants should be dealt with in the three months before the start of works. During the course of the Drainage compensation for those affected by changes to dykes, etc., was to be met by assessors. The Participants, through Cornelius Vermuyden, had legal rights to drain Hatfield Chace but not the commons of the manors of Wroot, Finningley, Misterton and the Isle of Axholme. We are told that 'certain persons did claim common of pasture in sundry of the said grounds and therefore the Crown undertook to issue a Commission to enable claimants to treat with such commissioners by way of composition in land or money, concerning the same'.[3]

The degree of protest against the reclamation varied between localities. In Hatfield Manor the Court judgement of 1630 had largely satisfied the inhabitants. In Fishlake and Sykehouse a measure of grudging satisfaction had been given by bank raising, but more substantial support for their cause was provided by the Order in Council enforcing the cutting of Dutch River. It was in the Manor of Epworth and adjacent areas of Axholme that the strongest feelings were aroused.

Much land which had been pastured by the local farmers had been taken for reclamation. It was offered back as arable land for renting but as such it was not attractive to stock farmers. They has lost valuable meadow land and thus winter fodder, and the result was that fewer stock could be kept. The flooding of land in winter had been a normal phenomenon which left a fertile layer of warp. But the inefficient new drainage had produced excessive flooding in summer and winter with no fertiliser benefit. There was also a loss of fishing and fowling, although sometimes compensation was paid. The fisheries of Crowle were allocated 40 ha (100 acres) of land in place of lost fishing.

However, the effect of the Great Drainage was to undermine the social and economic structure of the Isle of Axholme. The commoners showed their objections by a combination of lawful and unlawful means. They had been disinclined to seek redress from the appointed commission but they brought legal actions, raising funds by local appeals. King Charles endeavoured to block such actions by forbidding fund raising. Substantial compensation was obtained (in, for example, Fishlake and Sykehouse) by some individuals and by local groups, though less often by the commoners. Similarly injunctions secured the unblocking of the old Idle River in 1634 and the sealing of the Adlingfleet arm of the Don.

Even while the main reclamation was in progress frequent attacks were made by Islonians (natives of the Isle of Axholme) upon banks, sluices and machinery. In 1631 a number of rioters were apprehended and were convicted by the Court of Star Chamber, suffering heavy fines. Robert Portington, a Justice of the Peace, of Barnby-on-Don instigated disturbances and further unrest occurred in the area of Epworth South Moor and Butterwick Moor in 1636. The local people claimed rights of common to 5,420 ha (13,400 acres) in those places and elsewhere, and they were not without just cause. A commission headed by Sir John Banks heard the arguments in 1636 and awarded a total of 2,830 ha (7,000 acres) of land to the commoners.[4] With the same award the Participants were ordered to pay £400 to purchase raw materials to enable the poor people of Epworth, Owston and Belton to make sackcloth, cordage and similar products. This domestic industry was already in being and help for it was to compensate for losses of fishing and fowling.

In 1636 Charles I leased to Cornelius Vermuyden the third part of the improved lands awarded to him in the original contract, such lands being situated in Epworth, Belton, Haxey, Gringley, Misterton, Snaith, Cowick, Rawcliffe and Crowle.[5] Vermuyden was to pay a total of £743.17s per annum for these lands. However, it appears that securing a quick operating profit from land holdings by farming or renting was proving extremely difficult for the Participants. Vermuyden very quickly transferred his new Crown land acquisition to Philip, Earl of Pembroke and Montgomery, and to Sir Richard Pye, for the Duke of Buckingham. He also sold shares in other land to Sir James Cats, who, in turn sold to Sir John Gibbon. This land included the manor of Hatfield, Fishlake, Thorne, Stainforth, Dowsthorpe (Sykehouse) and Hatfield Parks. For some 770 ha (1,900 acres) of land Gibbon would pay £200.1.8d to the Crown. Vermuyden then disposed of all of his remaining reclaimed land to various purchasers, who accepted the responsibility of paying a fee-farm rent (fixed ground rent) to the Crown.

It is significant that after only ten years of involvement Sir Cornelius Vermuyden had virtually washed his hands of the Hatfield adventure. He transferred his interest and enthusiasm elsewhere, ultimately to the Bedford Level but immediately to the Dove Gang lead mine in Derbyshire. Here he partnered his old friend and supporter at Court, Sir Robert Heath, though Vermuyden's financial worth at this time must have been minimal. By 1634 Vermuyden had failed to pay debts to the extent that he had been committed on several occasions to 'The Fleet', the London debtors' prison. His position had not been helped by the costs of lawsuits with his own countrymen, including Sir Philibert Vernatti and Sir James Cats, as well as others.

Vermuyden's wife was a daughter of All Saints Lapps of London and their family consisted of Cornelius junior, John, Sarah, Catherine and Adriand. Though the fact is disputed in the *Dictionary of National Biography* of 1893, it is believed that Cornelius junior entered the Parliamentary Army under General Fairfax where he held the rank of Captain.[6] He was initially stationed in the Fens but may have been present at the battle of Marston Moor. For reasons not altogether clear, he resigned his commission and left for The Netherlands before the battle of Naseby of 1645. One of the Vermuyden daughters married a certain John Thorpe of Thorne, and as late as 1888 a descendant, a Mrs Kilham, lived at Mexborough, South Yorkshire.[7]

Vermuyden had taken no part in the construction of Dutch River and his subsequent *magnum opus* was the Fenland drainage for the Duke of Bedford. He had purchased for £5,000 and subsequently drained Malvern Chase in Worcestershire and later he purchased 1,620 ha (4,000 acres) on Sedgemoor in Somerset for £12,000, selling it after reclamation.

Meanwhile the Participants had difficulties both in meeting their drainage rates, or scots, and in paying their workers. More than 1,000 workmen obtained a 'Commission of Rebellion', empowering them to arrest on court order any employer in arrears of wages or to sequester the land of any such employer who had fled! By 1630 the Participants had paid £16,800 into the Exchequer together with a fee-farm rent of £3,036 per ha (£1,228.17s per acre). They had spent some £175,000 on the drainage works and now 'enjoyed' title to 9,700 ha (24,000 acres) of land.[8] The insoluble problem for them was to realise this wealth in liquid form, in other words to generate a cash flow.

Hatfield Manor, owned so briefly by Vermuyden, passed through several hands after 1630. During an important period the famous Sir Arthur Ingram became Lord of the Manor.[9] His ancestor, Hugh Ingram of Thorpe on the Hill, near Leeds, made a huge fortune from linen drapery in London in Elizabethan times. Sir Arthur became Comptroller of the Customs of London, but failed in a large trading speculation. Following this débâcle he was transferred to the post of Surveyor of the King's Alum Mines. He became member of Parliament for York, building a mansion there. In 1622 he purchased and extensively altered Templenewsham House in Leeds. Sir Arthur was to be an important supporter of the Participants' cause at a critical juncture.

The incompleteness and the inefficiency of the Drainage were the source of much irritation to the towns and villages affected. Local authorities in Nottinghamshire petitioned the Privy Council, alleging damage, and a ruling was made against the Participants. The same types of complaint were made by 11 Yorkshire townships at Doncaster Sessions in 1635. The case was referred to the Council of the North and thence to the Privy Council. The Court of Chancery was also involved where debt repayments had not been met.

A controlling brief over the whole area was kept by the Commission of Sewers, comprising up to 80 local 'gentlemen' who regulated reclaimed lands and made recommendations. It acted virtually as a Government authority. The members sat for a four-year term of office, and they included 20 from each of the counties of Yorkshire, Lincolnshire and Nottinghamshire, together with 20 representatives of the Participants. A clerk was appointed and the meetings were usually held in Doncaster. The officers, who took an oath, included a Surveyor of Sewers and an 'Expenditor'. The Chairman was elected and a bailiff carried out court warrants in a manner comparable to that of a court of justice.

An example of the work of the Commission of Sewers was the commissioning of a new cut of a width of 20 m to discharge into the Trent from Misterton, Gringley and Everton to relieve Bykersdyke at Cornley Nook. Only about 2 km of this course had been dug before obstruction by landowners stopped the work. On another occasion the Commission, sitting at Bawtry in 1637, ordered that land owned by John Gibbon and others be sold to pay drainage labour costs.

Notes

1. Tomlinson, J. (1882), op. cit.
2. Ibid.
3. Stonehouse, W.B. (1839), op. cit.

4. Wainwright, J. (1826), op. cit.
5. Robinson, C.B. (1861), op. cit.
6. Lee, S. (ed.), *Dictionary of National Biography* (1893).
7. Mrs Kilham, née Jenny Thorpe, was born at Fishlake on 2 March 1788, the daughter of John Thorpe, farmer. This man was the great grandson of John Thorpe who lived at Thorne during the Drainage and who married a daughter of Cornelius Vermuyden (Le Moine, H.G.B. (1889), op. cit.).
8. The amount varies between records: de la Pryme gives £300,000, Read, £55,825.
9. Tomlinson, J. (1882), op. cit.

15 The Effect of the Civil Wars

The English Civil Wars involved a confrontation between an absolute monarch (and later his son) who was convinced of his divine right to rule, and a Parliament aggressively asserting new powers to control high offices of state and generally endeavouring to thwart royal prerogatives.[1] The Hatfield Chace venture was the result of the King's initiative in seeking a source of wealth for his political aims. Thus, in the first polarisation of interests in the Hatfield-Axholme area, the Participants and the foreign settlers sided with Royalists while the Islonians promptly aligned themselves with the Parliamentary cause. This division coincided with a national partition since the York area was strongly Royalist while Lincoln was Parliamentarian.

The hostile attitude of the Axholme commoners received new vigour when war broke out in 1642. They raised two companies of foot soldiers, comprising 495 men, for the Parliamentary forces. The Participants, for their part, contributed one troop of cavalry for the King. In The Levels the initiative was seized by the commoners to create disorder and to appropriate land from the Participants. In the first year of the war they are said to have spread a rumour that Sir Ralph Hansby with Royalist troops was about to invade the Isle from the south.[2] On this pretext they broke down the Snow Sewer flood gates and the sluice at Misterton Soss on the Idle. The district became flooded and great damage ensued, quoted by some authorities as amounting to £20,000 in value. Probably at a later date, damage was also caused at Althorpe, Goole and Turnbridge. The Participants, the main sufferers, were already in a poor financial state, with some already returning to The Netherlands. Nevertheless they made valiant efforts to stem the tide of disasters. According to one account the Dutch settlers had taken steps to hire soldiers to resist rent collectors and to raise a local tax to meet the cost. Gabriel Vernatti had had his horses and cattle impounded after obstructing collectors. Thereupon Marcus van Valkenburgh proceeded to Doncaster and hired 15 soldiers from the military depot to rescue the stock! In a belated attempt to confer legality on their action they then obtained a warrant from a Justice of the Peace to indict the collectors, who were subsequently acquitted. These same two Dutchmen were also reported to have refused to pay poor labourers for work done.[3]

Other attempts to prevent seizures for debt were made by the Participants. In one case they served writs of *certiorari* against collectors and sheriffs.[4] Matthew Brunyee was convicted of contempt of court following distraint on his property for debt. He was committed to York Castle on remand.[5]

Believing the national situation to be moving in their favour, some Epworth commoners sought legal authority to recover former grazings but failed in their attempts. Others seized land illegally. The Idle and Snow Sewer sluices were repaired by the Sheriff of Lincoln and 1,620 ha (4,000 acres) were restored. However a rabble army of 400 villagers promptly destroyed the dams once more. The Participants instituted legal action for recovery, proceedings that continued for many years. By this time each side had secured an agent or 'solicitor' to present its separate case and to direct local action. The commoners' first solicitor was Thomas Vavasour, Squire of Belwood and member of an ancient Axholme family. He was followed by John Pinder of Owston. A more notable officer was Daniel Noddel who initiated land and stock seizure while the Participants' case was *sub judice*. Noddel was also able to summon outside aid to the commoners' cause when a ruling by the Exchequer Chamber found for the Participants in 1650. The aid was in the remarkable person of John Lilburne, late of the Parliamentary army, and with him came a Major Wildman. This group ignored the Exchequer ruling, and with military assistance destroyed 50 buildings in Sandtoft village, and on neighbouring farms laid waste crops on 1,375 ha (3,400 acres) of the disputed land. There appears to have been a sharing out of the land whereby Lilburne and Wildman were to be rewarded for their efforts with 800 ha (2,000 acres) of the 3,000 ha (7,400 acres) secured by forcible seizure. Noddel was to receive 80 ha (200 acres). At Crowle, J. Margrave and George Stovin also secured land in similar fashion. Lilburne repaired and then occupied the Minister's house at Sandtoft and proceeded to utilise the church as a stable! The appearance of Lilburne in Hatfield Chace at this time is not a little surprising, and the intrusion justifies a diversionary sketch of this mercurial personality.[6]

John Lilburne attained the rank of Lieutenant Colonel in the Parliamentary forces but resigned when he found he could not sign the Covenant, a requirement for joining the New Model Army. He was at all times a storm petrel in the Parliamentary cause. He narrowly escaped a sentence of death by the King's Justices on a charge of treason, after being captured at a Brentford skirmish in 1642. He became involved in a strenuous demand for liberty of speech and action of a type hitherto unknown and unacceptable to any authority at the time. After his release, following threats to the King of Parliamentary reprisals, he became the unofficial leader of a campaign for the 'Birthright of all Englishmen', and in 1645 created the Leveller Party with William Walwyn. He had already been imprisoned between 1638 and 1640 for circulating seditious pamphlets. He was again in Newgate Prison in 1645 for attacking Parliamentarian Speaker Lenthall. Released from Newgate he continued to be a thorn in the side of authority and was repeatedly imprisoned and liberated. He could count on a degree of support from sympathisers and he was an inveterate pamphleteer. During a brief peaceful period in his career he espoused the causes of others who felt themselves aggrieved. Amongst these were the Tenants of the Manor of Epworth. The acceptance of at least the promise of a substantial land reward might appear to be out of character in a man committed unselfishly to help his fellow men. However, John Lilburne was no simple character. He had energetically tried to obtain considerable compensation for wrongs which he claimed to have suffered. Furthermore, in 1652, he was found to have made 'false, malicious and scandalous' claims in a case involving his uncle. There is no evidence that he ever received the proffered land. When he died in 1657 a writer of the day suggested the following epitaph for this complex, extroverted character:

Is John departed, and is Lilburne gone
Farewell to Lilburne and farewell to John
But lay John here, lay Lilburne here about
For if they ever meet they will fall out.

Despite the general mêlée the Participants persisted in their legal claim and in 1653 at last secured a judgement in their favour. This was followed by a ruling that the commoners be apprehended and punished for the damage done. To this Noddel entered a plea to delay such proceedings, while the general atmosphere of unrest continued. By this time both the Participants and the Crown had lost *de facto* occupancy of virtually all of their land allocation. It is also probable that the drainage works were damaged and operating very inefficiently.

But then, in 1655, another striking personality took the stage on the side of the Participants: Nathaniel Reading.[7] Reading was born in 1612 and after a good education was called to the Bar in the Inns of Court. He married Arabella Churchill, who was a sister to Sir Wynston Churchill and an aunt to John Churchill, the first Duke of Marlborough. A Roman Catholic, he was a man of strong character having been involved in a number of stormy events in the capital before coming to Hatfield Chace. His first commission was to collect arrears of royal rents in the Hatfield Levels 'for the delinquency of George Villiers, Duke of Buckingham'. There he encountered the Participants and offered to assist them in their land problems. They were unable to reach agreement as to employment terms, and so Reading approached the 'opposition' and was briefly engaged by the commoners as their 'solicitor'. Finally he was persuaded by Sir Arthur Ingram, Lord of Hatfield Manor, to become agent for the Participants. Thus in 1655, at a salary of £200 per annum, he commenced the energetic collection of rents, this time from the tenants of the Participants. In 1656 the commoners appealed to the courts against such rents, but an official enquiry headed by General Whalley found for the Participants.

For a time there was a relative calm, but Reading, with an accurate appraisal of likely events, recruited a small force, including, we are told, a 'chirurgeon'. Violence broke out again in 1656 and in the next five years Reading's 'army' was involved in 31 pitched battles, mainly against Islonians from Epworth and men from Misterton and Gringley in the southern area. Using his legal knowledge Reading brought successful actions during this period, but complete peace in the area was not achieved.

In spite of his Hatfield obligations Reading retained an interest in

London's political affairs. In 1678 Titus Oates, a roguish fanatic, spread details of a 'Popish Plot' aimed at assassinating Charles II, the reigning monarch. Reading acted as counsel for certain peers sympathetic to the Catholic cause, and because of this association he was pilloried and fined for having 'suborned the King's Evidence'.

Meanwhile in the Hatfield-Axholme area rioting was again on the increase. In 1688 a new attack was made on Sandtoft during which the church was burned down and other destruction effected. A temporary agreement between Participants and commoners was made in 1691, but trouble again flared when Reading claimed £3,000 in rent arrears. The riot was led by a Mrs Popplewell and not only were Reading's barns, cattle and crops destroyed but he himself barely escaped with his life when his house was burned down. He was then nearly 80 years of age but he refused to bring proceedings against the offenders, merely agreeing to accept £600 in damages. From this time it appears that open rioting declined and perhaps Nathaniel Reading had played a significant part in the long struggle for pacification. He died at Belton in 1712, aged 100.

Of the original Participants none was left after 1719 although their interests and obligations remained. Nathaniel's son Robert, a Lieutenant Colonel in Clayton's Regiment, succeeded his father as agent. He lived at Sandtoft in the house that replaced his father's residence and he farmed nearby. During some disturbances in 1714 the writer, George Stovin, recalled seeing soldiers encamped on the farm to protect land and stock. In the next year Robert took part in the action to defeat the 'Old Pretender', Charles Edward Stewart. The Riot Act, passed in 1711, provided for firm action by the military in the event of insurrections and this was a strong deterrent in the Hatfield area, even though the reasons for its enactment arose elsewhere.

A final lawsuit was brought by the commoners against the Participants in 1719 with Robert Reading appearing for the defence. The action failed and thus the original third of the reclaimed area, together with the acquisitions from the Crown by Gibbon and Corselis, fell to the successors of the original '57'.

Notes

1. Wedgwood, C.V., *The King's War* (Collins, 1958).
2. Korthals-Altes, J. (1925), op. cit.
3. Stovin, G. (1752), op. cit.
4. Writ of *certiorari*: this requires an inferior tribunal to transmit its record to the High Court, so that an applicant may have speedy justice.
5. Lee, S. (1893), op. cit.
6. Ibid.
7. Korthals-Altes, J. (1925), op. cit.

16 Post Reclamation: Problems and Remedial Work

The deficiencies of the original drainage scheme were soon compounded by the damage caused in the riots and sabotage of the years following 1630. Sluices were destroyed, banks broken, and any hope of quick returns from farming the reclaimed land promptly disappeared. Later in the century there were records of 'natural' floods which caused much damage. The Thorne district suffered destruction of land and property by floods on 15 January 1681 and again on 27 April 1682. In 1687 great areas of Hatfield Chace and Axholme were affected by devastating floods. On 13 December 1688 another inundation occurred which is said to have broken banks in many places from Dutch River in the north to the Idle in the south. At that time Fishlake and Skyehouse, always prone to flooding from the Don's west bank, were particularly affected. Far to the south the Gainsborough district fell victim to the same flood. A smaller inundation occurred in 1701.

The only major remedial scheme to be carried through in the 17th century was Dutch River, which has already been referred to. A new sluice to the outfall of this river at Goole was installed in 1651, but this was subsequently destroyed when flooding converted the double channels into one river. It was not replaced. To ease flooding problems in the southern area a new river to connect the Idle with the Trent was proposed but never completed. Some developments took place after 1717 in the district lying between Crowle and the Trent.[1] In the Middle Ages the Paupers Drain had been cut to drain this area and a new sewer, crossing the old drain, was excavated to serve Crowle, Eastoft and Luddington. This was to discharge at a new Trent outfall, Keadby, somewhat north of the Althorpe sluice. In 1761 this new sluice burst, presumably at high tide, with devastating results for the hinterland.

The area of carr land in the parishes of Misteron, Everton and Gringley was particularly liable to flooding from the Idle. The Soss (sluice) was installed in 1630 to control the tidal Trent but the problem was complicated by the need for navigation to Bawtry, for which a lock was provided in 1670. In 1763 the distinguished civil engineer, John Smeaton, was called in by the Participants to advise on the situation and he recommended the construction of an additional sluice.

After many years of inadequate attempts at a solution a Mother Drain was constructed between 1769 and 1803. This drain was closely parallel to the Idle on the South side and it collected water from the carrs and, eventually with the help of steam power, discharged directly into the Trent.

Smeaton also advised the Participants in 1771 upon the problems arising to the north of the Idle.[2] A bank had broken at Idle Stop and severe flooding had occurred throughout the district. This area was also drained by the Snow Sewer, and Smeaton was responsible for lowering the sill by 10 cm at the outfall of this drain into the Trent. Smeaton also reported upon the state of the River Torne and, for the first time, we are provided with exact data as to levels. The 'Double Rivers' discharging into the Trent could be effective only at below high tide periods. Smeaton found that at a point 4.425 km from the sluice the water level was lowered by only 22.8 cm during a full tidal period. Land around Tunnelpits was most 'oppressed with water' with the water level in the Torne 76.2 cm above land level and 2.73 m above the level of Althorpe sluice sill.

Smeaton regarded Misson Deeps and the area around Bull Hassocks as the most difficult parts to drain. This is a flat area remote from the outfall 'near to that part of the level bordering upon New Idle, where the water runs indifferently towards the Tunnel and so to Althorpe or towards Snow Sewer and so to Ferry sluice according as it makes its best descent'. In fact, water in the New Idle was allowed to run only two days a week. Work advised to improve the Snow Sewer was not carried out. Smeaton was fairly satisfied with the New Idle gradient of 0.887 m in 3.218 km towards Dirtness. He recommended a new Torne relief river and the broadening and deepening of the outfalls at Althorpe. This proposal was turned down when the commoners refused to make any contribution to the cost.

To improve the general discharge Smeaton recommended a new river with an outfall at Waterton, some 8 km downstream of Althorpe; this would also incorporate a 'surplus water basin'. However, this and most of his other recommendations were not put into effect.

From around 1760, the date generally accepted as the beginning of the so-called Agricultural Revolution, much common land in England was enclosed. Though it was a century before the whole of Axholme was so affected, Epworth Common was subjected to an Enclosure Act in 1795. Such a radical partitioning of the land required more complete drainage and the award included £20,000 to make the necessary improvements. The Act, which dealt with the Isle of Axholme Commons, named nine General Commissioners to oversee the enclosures.[3] Joseph Young and Jonathan Teale were appointed Surveyors, while William Jessop, a distinguished engineer associated with the drainage of Holderness, and Joseph Hodskinson became the official Engineers. The Participants' Engineer at this time was Samuel Foster and it is clear that some of the proposals of Jessop and Hodskinson were incorporated with his own projects. These provisions resulted in breaking the Idle Stop-Dirtness line of the New Idle at Tunnelpits and constructing a new channel for that river parallel to the Torne but at a lower level. This drain was discharged in a separate outfall upstream of the existing Althorpe sluice. By means of a valve New Idle water could be diverted at Tunnelpits towards Dirtness, thence discharging at Vermuyden's original Althorpe outfall.

At this time the Isle or Folly Drain was constructed. Jessop had proposed that this drain should start at Idle Stop and utilise the re-excavated course of the original River Idle, passing, by a tunnel, under the Snow Sewer. It would then proceed around the north-west side of the Isle following approximately the same direction as the New Torne but discharging in an entirely new outfall at Derrythorpe, south of Althorpe. This was carried out by 1801 but the Idle Stop-Tunnelpits section does not appear to have been successful. Later the Folly Drain commenced near Greenholme Bank and, collecting water from north of Haxey Carr, eventually joined the main confluence at Pilfrey for Keadby.

During this 'Jessop-Hodskinson-Foster' period of activity the drainage of the southern part of Haxey parish received much attention. Although the Monkham Drain had long existed in this area the new Ferry Drain was cut closely parallel to and north of Snow Sewer to discharge at a new outfall near Owston Ferry, now known as Drain Head. There was a further proposal to drain land between Snow Sewer and the River Idle by means of a sewer which passed under the Snow Sewer and would discharge into the Ferry Drain. It is not certain whether this work was actually carried out: today no trace remains.

Figure 7 Pilfrey: converging water courses

Not to scale

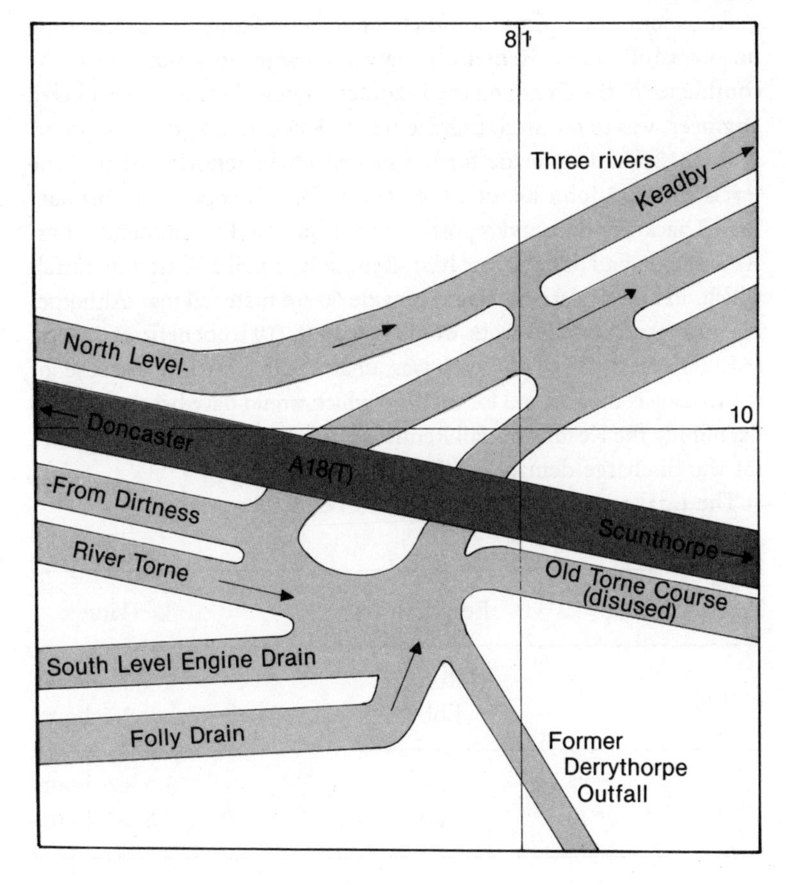

The Kelfield Catchwater taking upland water east of Epworth to the Trent and the Butterwick Drain both date from this period (1787-1803). Foster was especially concerned with the northward outfalls and was later responsible for diverting the rivers emerging eastwards from Dirtness into the Keadby outfall. Some idea of the complicated system which emerged can be seen today at Pilfrey (Figure 7).

Despite this bold attempt its results were disappointing. Foster appears to have made no attempt to use any form of pumping, nor did any of his successors do so until 1828. Foster also reversed the flow of Snow Sewer into the New Idle, but this change appears to have been of limited duration.[4]

At about this time another engineer, Stone, was pleading unsuccessfully for a Trent Falls main discharge, to a point near the confluence of the Trent and the Humber. George Leather, a Leeds civil engineer, was to return to this theme in 1830 with no greater support.

In 1812 Thackray made further surveys of the sensitive areas of the levels. In 1813 John Rennie, the greatest British engineer of his day, used Thackray's data and reported his findings and recommendations. As Smeaton had done before him, Rennie favoured a Waterton outfall which, in his calculations, would provide 60 cm more fall than Althorpe. He estimated that this work would cost £80,719 to benefit 13,760 ha (34,000 acres). This proposal was unacceptable mainly because of inadequate compensation for the land which would have been sacrificed. Examining the Keadby outfall Rennie found the situation unsatisfactory for the discharge demanded (Figure 8).

The tidal restrictions were found to be as follows:

Tide	Run/Ebb	Time
Spring	Run	2.5-3 hours
	Ebb	9-9.5 hours
Neap	Run	3.5-4 hours
	Ebb	8-8.5 hours

Figure 8 Keadby Discharge, 1813

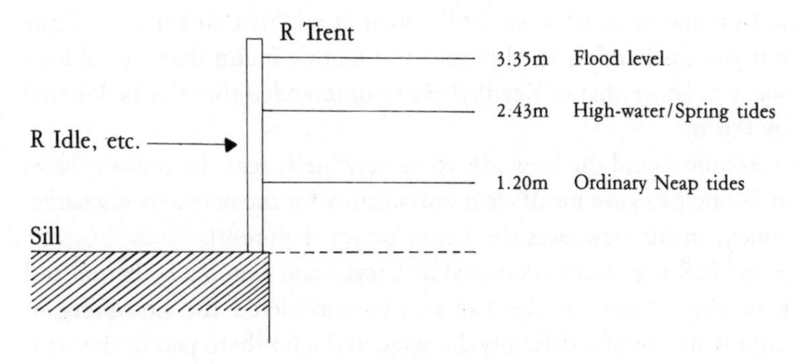

Figure 9 Tunnelpits, 1813

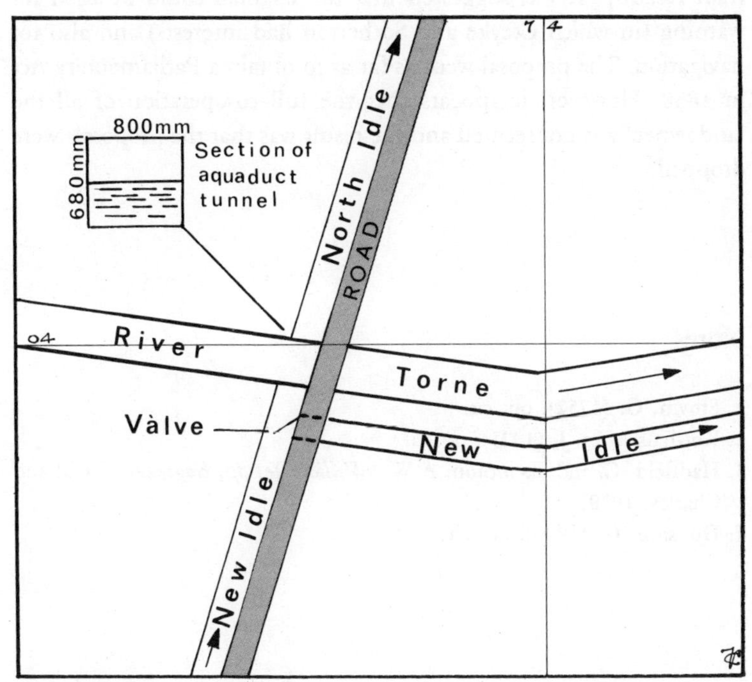

Not to scale

Source: Rennie

However, Rennie reported that the doors were open for only 4.5 hours at best and at worst were hardly open at all. At that time the Torne was still discharging at Althorpe, and Rennie found that the sill level was 1 m above that of Keadby! He recommended that this be lowered by 0.6 m.

Rennie found the New Idle to be very inefficient. Its two-way valve at Tunnelpits gave insufficient opportunity for the northerly discharge, which, in his view, was the better outlet (Figure 9).

In 1828 a syndicate promoted by Creyke and Admiral Sotherton and with the support of the Participants considered the possibility of improving the unsatisfactory drainage in the northern part of the area. They recommended a new outfall for the north level at Ousefleet. From Dirtness this was calculated to provide a 1.2 m lower discharge point than Keadby. It was suggested that the channel could be used for warping (in which Creyke and Sotherton had interests) and also for navigation. The proposal went as far as to obtain a Parliamentary Act in 1830. However, it appears that the full co-operation of all the landowners was not secured and the result was that the proposals were dropped.

Notes

1. Stovin, G. (1752), op. cit.
2. Korthals-Altes, J. (1925), op. cit.
3. Hadfield, C. and Skempton, A.W., *William Jessop, Engineer* (David and Charles, 1970).
4. Dunston, G. (1909), op. cit.

17 The Advent of Steam Power

In 1828 there were severe summer floods due to high levels in the Trent which prevented the opening of sluices. The disaster provided the occasion for introducing steam power into the area and an engine and pump were installed south of the Idle to lift water from Misterton Carr.

At this point it might well be asked why pumping was not used before in the Hatfield-Axholme area and what means would have been available to assist the gravitational drainage had they been called upon. There is no complete answer to the first question except that some simple, hand or animal operated devices were probably utilised. It would appear that the engineers were confident that gravity methods would suffice. Certainly, until the advent of steam, there was no power source available to ensure that outfalls discharged at all states of the tide. It might be thought that the use of windmills could have facilitated the movement of field drainage water to small arterial drains and, by a second lift, into the main rivers. However, the Dutch drainers were no mere novices and it is safe to assume that they had no better alternative to the methods they employed.

Windmills, as we have seen, date from the 15th century in The Netherlands, and they had probably been introduced into England by 1600. In *The Drainage of the Fens* H.C. Darby states that in the early 17th century there were notices of patents for engines for raising water and draining surrounding grounds.[1] Windpumps were in general use by the latter half of the 17th century. Blith, writing in 1652 on 'engines', states: 'and there plant a water-engine, which may be wrought either by the wind or by the strength of horse, yea, possibly by the strength of two or three men; which, if the compass of thy hand be not great, and thy water small, may be but a very inconsiderable charge'.[2]

In the Bedford Level windmills lasted for 150 years, and as late as 1852 there were still 220 from an original total of 700. But in Hatfield and Axholme the only mills were for grinding corn or colza oil! Pumping windmills operated either through a scoop-wheel fitted with paddles or buckets or through an Archimedean worm. The early steam powered pumps were of the scoop-wheel type and their use persisted through much of the 19th century.

In the Fens the first steam pumping engine was erected by the Littleport and Downham Drainage Board between 1819 and 1820. It was rated as of 30 nominal horse power (n.h.p.). Rennie, who was a personal friend of James Watt, had foreseen the possibilities of steam power as early as 1789.[3] In the Fens he encountered much prejudice on the part of Drainage Boards committed to windmills. In The Netherlands major reclamation schemes had had to wait for mechanical power and one of the first projects to benefit from steam was the Zuidplas Polder in 1839. The huge Haarlemermeer Polder of 20,000 ha was completed in 1852 using 27 steam engines, including a monstrous compound engine from Harvey's of Hayle in Cornwall.[4]

The earliest steam pumping engine to be employed outside the Fens was the 40 hp unit installed by Joseph Glynn in 1828 on the Mother Drain near Misterton Soss. In 1829 Lord Althrop purchased a steam engine for his estate at Wiseton on the Idle, near Gringley, Nottinghamshire. In 1839 a second engine was installed on the Misterton Soss, Mother Drain site. The two units coped successfully with the requirements until 1941 when a diesel set and a reorganised system was based at Gringley Carr.

In the Isle of Axholme Sir Robert Sheffield, on his estate between Epworth and the Trent, was an early user of the steam engine for pumping. One such was installed at Butterwick South Moor in 1837. Though not a total success it was not replaced by a more efficient machine until 1854. Meanwhile, in 1846, further steam units were installed on the same estate, one at Rush Carr and another at Newland Farm. In due course steam powered pumps were installed at the critical points of Bull Hassocks, covering the southern Isle of Axholme area, and of Dirtness, vital point in the North Levels (see cover photograph). The engines were originally low pressure, condensing beam or side-lever types of formidable dimensions. Each station included an engine house in the centre with boilers to one side (together with tall chimneys) and a huge scoop-wheel on the other. The whole station would have been built on piled foundations. Erected in 1858, the Bull Hassocks engine developed 40 n.h.p. and drove a scoop-wheel with a diameter of 9.1 m and a lift of 1.52 m.

The two Dirtness engines of 1867 were built at the famous Soho, Birmingham, works of James Watt. They were compound condensing beam engines each of 50 n.h.p. They were coupled to a crankshaft carrying a flywheel and pinion which geared into the scoop-wheel rim. The scoop-wheel weighed 81 tonnes and was 10.1 m in diameter. The cylinder diameter of each high pressure cylinder was 50.8 cm with a stroke of 1.33 m and the low pressure cylinder was almost 90 cm in diameter with a stroke of 1.83 m. The engine beams were enclosed in the massive engine house and there were four double flued boilers each 6.09 m long. The scoop-wheel rotated at four revolutions per minute to move over 1,200 tonnes of water per hour. The installed cost was £9,000.

At about the same time similar pumps were installed on Trentside at Sturton Soss, Torksey, Marton and Ravensfleet.[5] The scoop-wheel used at that time resembled a simple undershot water wheel, operating in reverse but power driven. The current of water was forced upwards instead of falling naturally downwards. The wheel was most often of cast iron and the flat boards, known as 'starts' and 'float boards' were readily replaceable. A typical scoop-wheel is shown in Figure 10.

By the mid-19th century the centrifugal pump came into use for land drainage. An early application was in the drainage of Whittlesey Mere, near Peterborough, in 1851. The vertical spindle centrifugal pump was used for large drainage schemes, while the horizontal spindle type was more suited to smaller workloads.[6] The invention of the compression ignition engine around 1890 provided the opportunity for a much more efficient pumping concept. However, the steam-based pumping systems persisted, their operators showing some of the resistance to change that had been displayed by the windmill engineers a century earlier. The James Watt engines at Dirtness and their scoop-wheel were only replaced by d.c. electric motors and pumps in 1928! (These were converted to a.c. motors with the extension of the National Grid in 1940). In extenuation it must be said that the general economic conditions in the area were unfavourable for heavy capital outlays at least for the first three decades of the 20th century. Today, with more prosperous

Figure 10 Scoop-wheel, steam driven, Trentside, 19th century

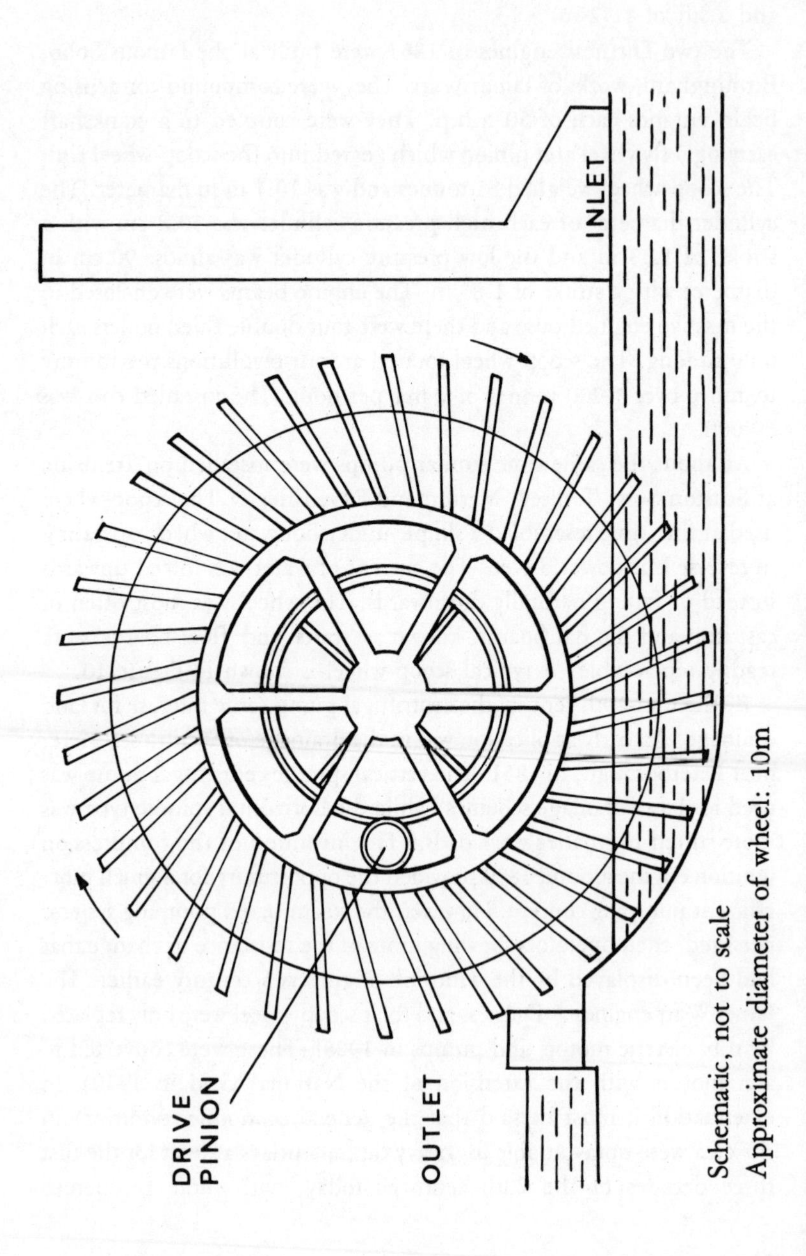

agricultural conditions, technical progress has been fully absorbed and the efficient, automatic, electric pump has been employed in most areas.

A steam driven pump which was installed in 1910 at the Ferry Pumping Station at Owston Ferry has been preserved by a local preservation society. The power units were built by Marshall's of Gainsborough and the pumps by Drysdale's of Glasgow. The set ran until 1964 when it was replaced by a diesel engine. In 1983 there was still one steam pump available at this station as a standby.

Notes

1. Darby, H.C. (1956), op. cit.
2. Blith, W., *The English Improver Improved* (1652).
3. Smiles, S, *Lives of the Engineers* (1862), Vol. II of 1904 edn.
4. The pumping station at Cruquius, with the Harvey engine, has been preserved as a museum and it includes a demonstration of the famous reclamation. It is 5 km south of Haarlem.
5. Gibbs, L. *Pumping Machinery in the Fenland and by the Trent* (1887).
6. Ibid.

18 Warping

Along with the attempts to improve the drainage of the Hatfield-Axholme area and so to raise the productivity of the soil, the practice of warping became increasingly important from the early years of the 19th century.[1]

'Warp' is the term applied to river or estuary borne sediment which, by natural or artificial means, settles on land after shallow flooding. The addition of such sediment has long been known to contribute to the fertility of the land. Special techniques appear to have been practised in Italy since the late 17th century, and systems were adopted around the Humber in the mid-18th century, probably first at Howden. Although the value of natural warp was appreciated, warping techniques were not employed in Hatfield Chace until long after the reclamation. By 1800, however, warping systems had become important means of improving low-lying land and especially peats. Before 1850 all peat lands up to 5 km west of the Trent had been warped.[2] Another 1,200 ha (3,000 acres) east of the Trent had also been so treated.[3]

While a good deal of eroded material from the East Yorkshire coast is moved southwards into the mouth of the Humber, the detritus of the Ouse and the Trent probably derives mainly from the basins of those rivers.[4] Nevertheless, the impact of the tide upon the Ouse and the Trent brings about a rapid deposition of suspended material.[5] The funnel-shaped nature of the estuary concentrates the force of the tidal flow and this accentuates the scouring of the banks, so producing new supplies of warp.

Warp consists of particles predominantly of the fine sand category with a mineral content which is both calcareous and micaceous. The soils resulting from warp application are distinctive. They fall within four main Soil Series:

1. Saltmarshe: fine, sandy, silty loam;
2. Blacktoft: silty, clay loam;

3. Walling fen: clay loam; and
4. Gowthorpe: silt clay.[6]

The first requirement was the availability of a controllable channel connecting with the main tidal rivers, the Trent or the Yorkshire Ouse. Natural channels or older drains could be employed, but often special cuts were necessary, such as the Swinefleet Warping Drain. This connects with the Ouse west of Swinefleet and penetrates in an almost straight line to the southern end of Thorne Waste. It was controlled by an outfall sluice and was used to reclaim peaty land. Dutch River was used directly as a warping source.

The procedure first called for the strong embankment of a rectangular area of land, known as a warping compartment, located alongside the warping drain. The slopes of this bank needed precise grading. Access of water to the compartment was closely controlled and the internal structure was carefully planned. The secret of success lay in allowing the incoming water to spread quickly and evenly over the land, securing a uniform deposit. Figure 11 illustrates typical layouts, but there were many variants. Return drains were carefully designed to enable the water to be drawn off completely between tides.

As a rough guide about 3.5 mm of warp was deposited with each tide, and under ideal conditions some 60-90 cm would result from one year's operation, though up to four years might be necessary for higher land. The weight of warp supplied annually was around 5,800 tonnes per ha (2,300 tons per acre), and the depth was about 45 cm. In most places where warping was completed the depth is more than 1 m thick. The area of land warped at one time was approximately 24-28 ha but 120 ha at one time was achieved on land served by the Amcoats and Keadby 'sea' sluices.

The reputation accruing to warping became accepted and the Enclosure Acts for Owston, Haxey, Epworth, Belton and Crowle prescribed this treatment in 1795 and subsequent Acts included Amcoats, Eastoft, Ealand, Luddington and Adlingfleet. When Crowle Manor was enclosed in 1813 the recipients warped 80 ha (200 acres) at the high cost of £61.12s per ha (£25 per acre). In 1854 the Snow Sewer Company was authorised by Parliamentary Act to take over and

Figure 11 Warping: typical warping compartments

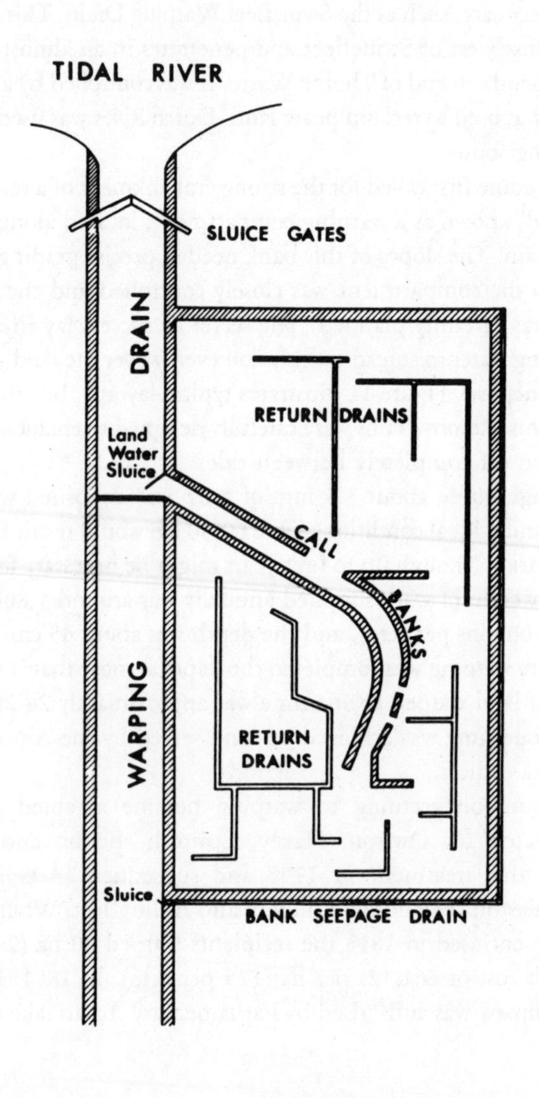

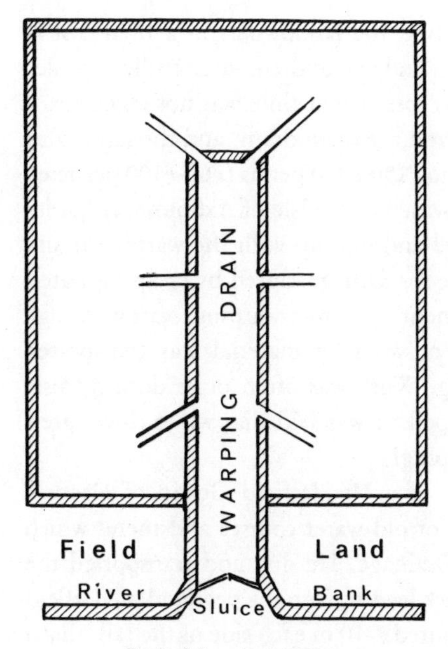
WARPING DRAIN
Field
Land
River
Sluice
Bank
TIDAL RIVER

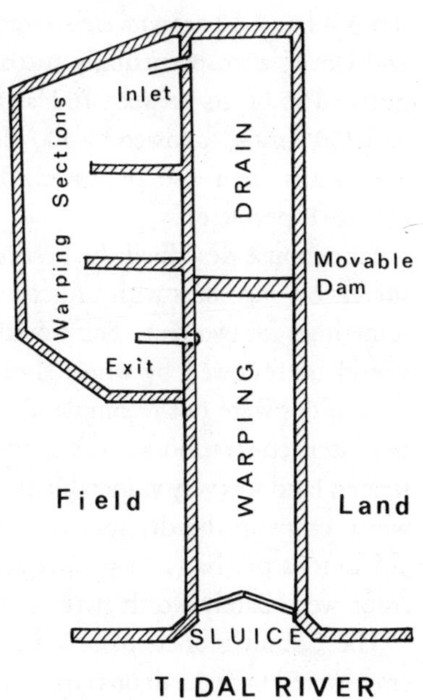
Inlet
Warping Sections
DRAIN
Movable
Dam
Exit
WARPING
Field
Land
SLUICE
TIDAL RIVER

warp adjacent land. This involved the landowners in a final cost of £37.12s per ha (£15.22 per acre), and one of them successfully appealed against the injunction. But this cost at that time was not excessive. It included the cost of the sluice and the main drain, and the land value could be raised from almost nil to £150-£250 per ha (£60-£100 per acre). Public warping drains were provided in the Isle of Axholme. Adjacent landowners could cut a channel and link up with the warping drain. However, they were responsible for damage caused by escaping water.

In addition to the 'compartment' system of warping, 'cart warping', or 'dry warping', was common, whereby material was transported overland for manual spreading. Work was often done during frosty weather or during a very dry spell. It was said that white clover grew 'spontaneously' after such warping!

Metcalfe describes the work of a Mr Hatfield Gossip of Hatfield Hall.[7] Gossip located the sites of old water courses and meres which had been terminated by the Drainage. He dug and transported the detritus using a light railway track leading into the peatland of Hatfield Moors. The material was distributed 7-10 m each side of the rails. Each day 3-4 ha (7-10 acres) were so treated, and good crops resulted. Grass and clover were particularly successful. On 47 ha (116 acres) Gossip fattened 95 beasts between 16 May and 25 August, along with 600 sheep and 250 lambs, followed by 400 old sheep up to 5 September. Turnips and beans were also produced. The cost was from £37-£45 per ha (£15-£18 per acre).

Stonehouse described the best rotations for warped land.[8] A typical succession was: oats with undersown clover and then grazing or hay, sometimes for two years. Salt would disappear during this period. These would be followed by wheat, beans, flax, and finally wheat.

Potatoes were not recommended in the early years of warped land, but later, cultivation was easier and the yields very satisfactory. Newly treated land was very vulnerable to a wet summer. Stonehouse instanced wheat crops in the dry season of 1826 being 1.5 m tall and yielding 3.4 tonnes per ha (27 cwts per acre), while in 1827, a wet year, the crops were barely worth harvesting.

The Commissioners of Sewers, during the Enclosures period, were empowered to make drains and ditches on common land as well as upon enclosed land. This included Participants' land and these owners were not asked to contribute to the cost of drainage of the commons. Surprisingly, the Participants were allowed to use the Isle of Axholme commoners' drains to warp their own land. This arrangement did not include the Epworth open fields, however.

There were a number of outstanding warping undertakers during the 19th century. Ralph Creyke of Rawcliffe House, Goole, was a well-known exponent.[9] He warped 174 ha (430 acres) in 1825 and received the Gold Medal of the Society for the Encouragement of the Arts in recognition. With Admiral Sotherton he was at one time involved in a scheme for warping 400 ha (1,000 acres) on Thorne Moors. This project was authorised by Act of Parliament in 1848, but protracted legal delays ensued and the work was never begun. Creyke had been responsible for the cutting of the Swinefleet Warping Drain whereby a considerable area of the Marshland was treated.[10] Another well-known operator was Makin Durham who was associated with the warping of Thorne Moors. His name is preserved in the Durham Warping Drain, connecting Thorne levels with the lower Don, south of New Bridge.

The work involved in the construction of warping drains was considerable and the opportunity was often taken of utilising drainage channels for this additional function. An example of this was the Snow Sewer. It is possible that excessive flooding may have been detrimental to some of the occupiers in such an area, although there is little evidence on this issue from contemporaneous or later records.

It is believed that the last warping to have been carried out in the Hatfield-Axholme region was just prior to the First World War when the Swinefleet Warping Drain was used for land reclaimed near Medge Hall, Crowle. On Humberside, warping took place at Yokefleet in 1948.

Notes

1. Thornton and Herapath, 'Improvement of Land by Warping', *Journal of the Royal Agricultural Society of England* (1850).

2. Marshall, W., 'Review of the Reports to the Board of Agriculture from the Northern Department of England' (1808), p. 387.
3. Thirsk, J., *English Peasant Farming* (1957), op. cit.
4. Wheeler, W.H., 'Source of Warp in the Humber', British Association Report: *Geological Magazine* (December 1901).
5. Heathcote, W.R., 'A Soil Survey of Warpland', *Journal of Soil Science*, 2 (1951), p. 144.
6. Soil Survey of England and Wales.
7. Metcalfe, B. (1960), op. cit.
8. Stonehouse, W.B. (1839), op. cit.
9. Creyke, R., 'Warping', *Society for Encouragement of the Arts*, Vol. 43 (1825).
10. Creyke, R., 'The Process of Warping', *Journal of the Royal Agricultural Society of England*, No. 5 (1844).

19 Navigation and Railways

Navigation

Before the Drainage much of the transport of the Chace and the Isle of Axholme was by boat.[1] In winter additional flooding improved the transit of people and goods. It was said that boats with 20 quarters of corn (about 4-5 tonnes) could pass to the (original) River Idle westwards across Haxey Carrs.[2] Between Westwoodside and Hatfield Woodhouse the water was 1 m deep throughout the year. The Great Drainage upset the main lines of communication and, in time, steps had to be taken to reinstate an efficient water transport system since no satisfactory roads existed. Indeed we know that a 'rule of the road' was that pedestrians give way to riders, such were the conditions of the surfaces. Not only was water transport important for the Chace and the Isle of Axholme but the large Yorkshire cities to the west and south were demanding access to the Humber ports.

In 1761 Brindley completed the Manchester-Worsley Canal for the Duke of Bridgewater and there followed a rush of canal construction throughout the north. The canal had considerable advantages over navigable rivers, especially the tidal courses. The depth was constant and the alignment planned; there were no currents and the canal could be regarded as an elongated lake.

In the Middle Ages the River Aire was navigable from the confluence with the Ouse to Knottingley, and in 1700 improvements made it navigable as far as Leeds.[3] From that time Selby became important to the industrial hinterland and in 1788 a canal was cut to link the Aire to this port. However, the port of Goole then made so much headway over Selby that in 1826 a new canal starting closely parallel to Dutch River was cut from Goole to Knottingley. Dutch River for more than a century had satisfied the transport needs of its day and had given the fillip to launch the town of Goole. However, the greatly superior facilities of a canal outdated those of a tidal river. The new canal formed part of the Aire and Calder system linking it with the immense industrial region of West Yorkshire and Lancashire.

The Stainforth-Keadby Canal was cut in 1792 with an eye to the South Yorkshire industries. At first it was run by an independent company but later became part of the Sheffield and South Yorkshire Navigation. Initially it joined the River Don but later connected with the Dun Navigation Canal, which was cut in stages up to 1751.[4]

Late in the history of canal building, in 1905, the New Junction Canal was constructed to link the Aire and Calder with the lucrative engineering and metal working industries of South Yorkshire. It crossed the parishes of Sykehouse and Fishlake to connect with the Dun Navigation near Barnby Dun.

On 1 June 1983 the British Waterways Board announced the reopening for freight traffic of the whole of the Sheffield and South Yorkshire Navigation network.

In the extreme south of the Hatfield-Axholme area the Chesterfield Canal with locks on the Trent near West Stockwith provided an early link with the South Yorkshire and Derbyshire industries. It was cut by Brindley in 1777 and proved to be profitable despite heavy construction and maintenance costs. Trade reached a peak in 1848 when the company was purchased by the Manchester and Lincoln Union Railway. Thereafter a familiar and inevitable decline took place.

In constructing canals special arrangements were necessary to preserve the already existing drainage systems. In the case of the Stainforth-Keadby Canal, 'soak dykes' had to be cut on each side to intercept local drains and to convey them to the Keadby outfall independently of the canal. When, in due course, metalled roads and railways were constructed similar arrangements were made. There were also 'peat canals' in use before coal displaced the local fuel. Boating Dyke is believed to have been part of such a canal. The layout of the canals in relation to the rivers is shown in Figure 12.

Figure 12 Navigation

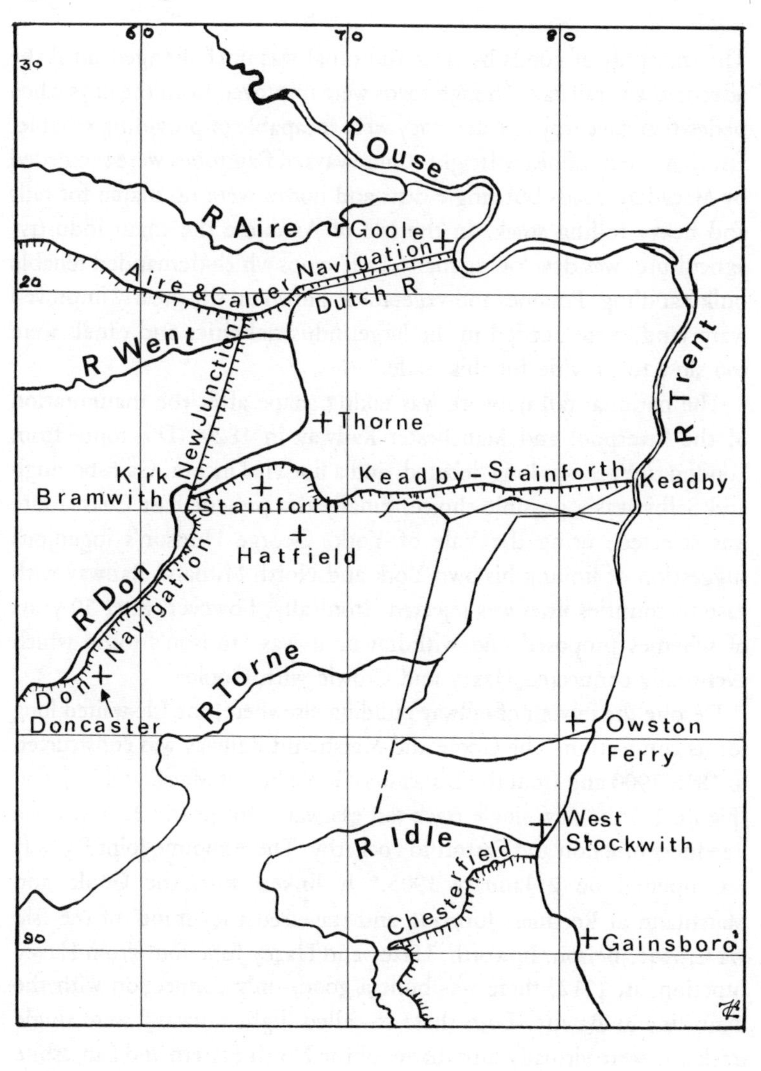

Railways

The transport of goods by river and canal was unchallenged until the advent of the railway. Though roads were improved from the days when pedestrian gave way to rider, they were incapable of providing reliable, fast movement of heavy freight. Causeways of flagstones were succeeded by Macadam roads but single carts and horses were no match for rails and heavy rolling stock. In the Isle of Axholme the main industry, agriculture, was developing many 'cash' crops which demanded reliable bulk handling. Potatoes and vegetables, grown on the greatly improved warp land, were needed in the large industrial cities and canals were too slow to provide for this trade.

The national rail network was taking shape after the inauguration of the Liverpool and Manchester Railway in 1829. The route from London to York was long debated, and a line via Lincoln, Gainsborough and Selby was a possible choice. Finally the present East Coast route was selected, using the Vale of York. George Hudson's ingenious suggestion of linking his own York and North Midland Railway with eastern counties lines was rejected. Ironically, however, after 50 years of schemes proposed and withdrawn, it was Hudson's route which eventually connected Haxey and Crowle with Goole.

Despite the fervour of railway building elsewhere, the Isle waited long for its connection. The Goole and Marshland Railway was constructed in 1898-1900 and from the Doncaster-Goole line at Marshland Junction (Figure 13) the new single track ran eastwards for nearly 22.5 km, via Reedness Junction and Eastoft to Fockerby. The Axholme Joint Railway was opened on 2 January 1905.[5] It linked with the Goole and Marshland at Reedness Junction and traversed the 'spine' of the Isle via Crowle, Belton, Epworth, Haxey and Haxey Junction. From Haxey Junction, in 1912, there was built a goods-only connection with the main line at Bawtry. Both these so-called 'light railways' were single track and were virtually subsidiaries of the North Eastern and Lancashire and Yorkshire Companies. Interestingly, the Axholme Joint had a branch line from Epworth via Sandtoft to Hatfield Moors to serve the Peat Moss Litter Works.

The competition with road traffic brought about the withdrawal of

Figure 13 Railways

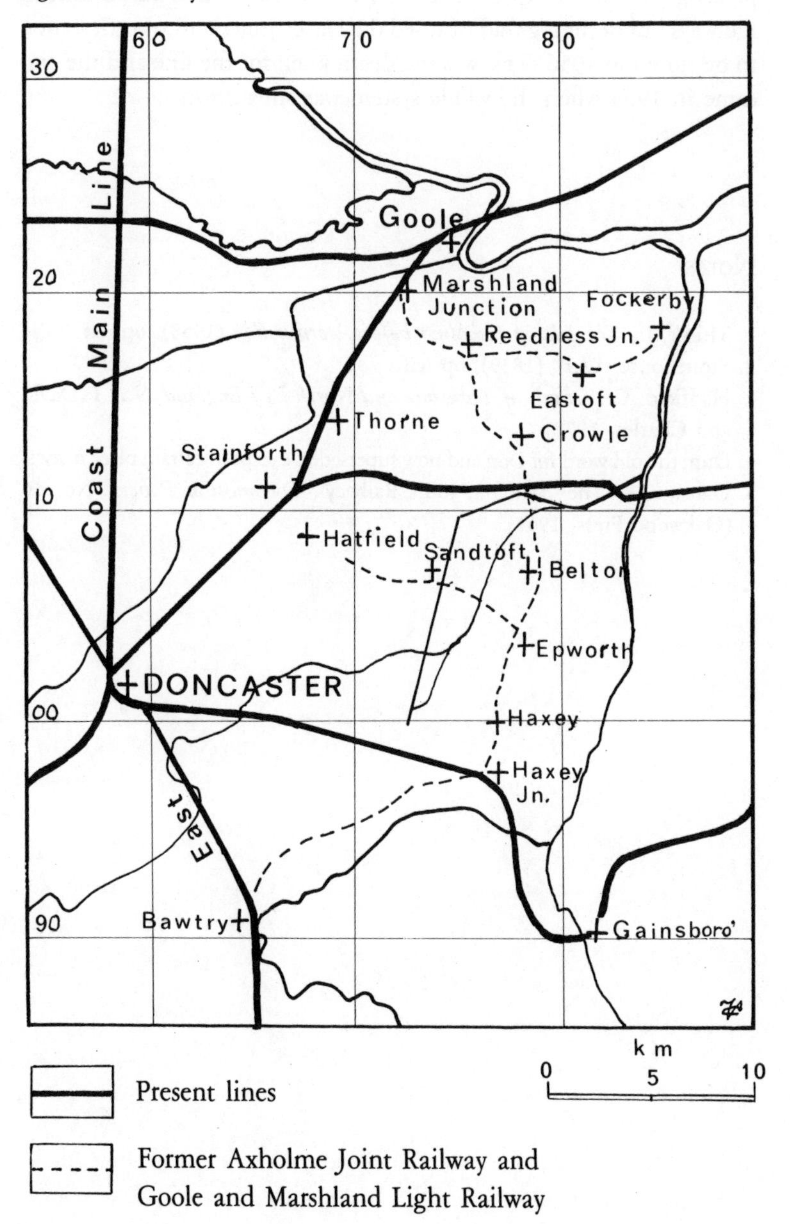

passenger services in 1933. In 1948 the network became part of British Railways but declining traffic caused the Haxey Junction-Epworth section to be closed in 1956. This was the death knell for the line and the end came in 1965 when the whole system was shut down.

Notes

1. Thirsk, J., *The Isle of Axholme before Vermuyden* (1953), op. cit.
2. Stonehouse, W.B. (1839), op. cit.
3. Hadfield, C., *Canals of Yorkshire and North East England*, Vol. I (David and Charles, 1972).
4. Dun: the old word for Don and now superseded except in certain place names.
5. Oates, G., 'The Axholme Joint Railway', *Locomotion Papers*, No. 16 (Oakwood Press, 1961).

20 The Act of Incorporation and 20th-Century Improvements to Drainage

Many years elapsed before any major works or significant reorganisation of the drainage systems took place. On 7 July 1862, 232 years after the prescribed time, an Act of Incorporation, establishing the status of the Participants, was passed.[1] A constitution was laid down, voting procedures established and a board of nine commissioners appointed. The new body was henceforth known as the Hatfield Chase Corporation. In due course the Catchment boards, and later the Water Authorities for the main rivers and the Internal Drainage Boards for arterial drainage, inherited the obligations which had been placed upon the Participants in 1626. The Hatfield Chase Corporation took active steps in two directions: it inaugurated the Dirtness steam pumping station, already described; and it assisted in the improvement of reclaimed land on the edge of Thorne Moor and reclaimed 200 ha of Hatfield Moor.[2] The inhabitants of Thorne had long enjoyed rights of turbary on the moor and as turf was removed they had gradually brought the underlying soil into cultivation. Such land required careful drainage and the new Corporation provided such help. Elsewhere on Thorne and Hatfield Moors warping had been employed in reclamation work. These moors were not subject to drainage rates but owners of peat workings have made arrangements over a long period for Drainage Authorities to remove surplus water.

In the Act of Incorporation the land owned by the Participants was quoted in a schedule. The totals were made up as in Table 6.

It was not until 1930 that any further change occurred. In that year a Land Drainage Act reached the Statute Book and ushered in a period of investment in river improvements. The Internal Drainage Boards, some of which had been in existence for many years, took part in the 'farm-to-river' stage of new, major drainage schemes. A general survey was made of the Hatfield-Axholme area and the locations of a number of new pumping station sites were selected. The key installation was

Table 6 Lands of the Participants at the time of the Act of Incorporation, 1862

District		Hectares (approximate)	Acres
South District:	Misson	831	2,053
	Wroot	1,035	2,559
	Finningley	35	86
	Blaxton	228	563
	Hatfield	5	12
Total		2,134	5,275
North District:	Hatfield	1,792	4,429
	Crowle	233	577
	Thorne	654	1,616
	Wroot	5	11
	Belton	41	101
Total		2,725	6,736
Outlying land:	Hatfield	166	410
	Thorne	400	989
	Adlingfleet	44	110
Total		610	1,510
Grand total		5,469	13,521

the construction of the Keadby pumping station, the logical culmination of Foster's work more than a century earlier. To this point were drawn the waters of all the channels from Bull Hassocks, the Torne and from the area north of Hatfield Moors. With the availability of adequate power such water could be discharged into the Trent at any state of the tide. The Keadby installation employed six Crossley Diesel engines each of 420 b.h.p. (313 kW). Operating Gwynne pumps the output was rated at 1,926 tonnes per minute.

The original outfall at Althorpe and the later discharge point at Derrythorpe were discontinued, and at Pilfrey all water was directed via Three Rivers to Keadby, without distinction as to source. After 1945 the station also dealt with seepage water from the North and South Soak Dykes bounding the Stainforth-Keadby Canal. The pumping stations at New Zealand and Medge Hall were installed, discharging water from the Thorne Moors and surrounding farms into the North Soak Dyke. Later the Wikewell pumping station was established to lift water into the South Soak Dyke. Subsequently the River Torne was deepened and flood banks and washlands improved. A pumping station was also installed at Candy Farm to service a total area of 2,460 ha (6,080 acres) of land on both sides of the river. The station deals with the so-called Low Grounds, south-west of Hatfield Moors. It utilises a syphon system under the Torne to collect water from drains south of the river.

North of Hatfield Moors, in an area of difficult, low levels a booster pump was added in 1939 to assist the flow of the Hatfield Waste Drain at Goodcop.

With the cessation of warping, Snow Sewer, or 'Park Drain', reverted to its simpler drainage function. A pumping station was installed near the New Idle (Park Drain Station) and at the Trent outfall a stand-by pump was provided for emergencies.

An elaborate means of dealing with the notorious New Idle Drain-River Torne intersection was put into operation in 1962 (Figure 14 and p.11, *bottom*). The station pumps water which has gravitated to this point from the North Idle Drain into the Torne. Four automatic electric pumps were installed and one of these draws water from the lower level soak drain and the South Idle Drain. A special device prevents a syphon action which otherwise might flood the low level with high-level water. In order to provide irrigation water for adjacent crops a penstock was installed connecting the River Torne with the low-level South Idle Drain. A culvert connects both sides of the low-level drain. It is of interest to compare the 1813 arrangement as found by Rennie (Figure 9) with the present system (Figure 14).

Figure 14 Tunnelpits, 1982

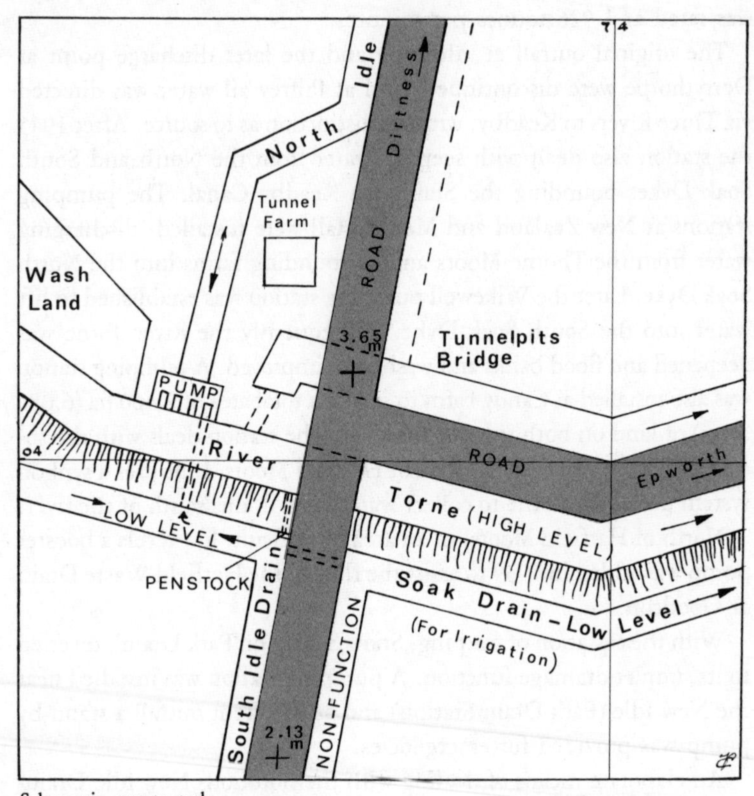

Schematic, not to scale

Notes

1. A Bill to set up a Corporation to run the Levels was defeated in the Commons in the 1660s.
2. Dunston, G. (1909), op. cit.

21 Recent Engineering Developments

Later developments in the area have been as a result of two important factors: first, the greater prosperity of agriculture which has enabled the financing of more elaborate work; and second, motorway construction, which has necessitated changes and additions to existing systems. The major development in the 19th century was the adoption of steam power. In parallel, the progress since 1939 has involved even greater dependence on power but in particular upon electricity. This energy source had many advantages over the intermediate use of diesel engines. Such power plants, while of much higher thermal efficiency than steam, required continuous manning, fuel supply and expensive maintenance. The electrically operated vertical axial flow (VAF) pump became a standard appliance for new major schemes while Archimedean screw pumps were sometimes employed in new Internal Drainage Board works.

The Trent River Board installed three pumps (two at 610 mm with a capacity of 1.26 m^3/sec and one at 380 mm with a capacity of 0.34 m^3/sec) at Greenholme in 1970, on behalf of the West Axholme Internal Drainage Board (IDB). Here, water is lifted from the Folly Drain into the South Level Engine Drain, which now gravitates to Pilfrey and thence to Keadby.[1] Formerly this water had to be coped with by the Bull Hassocks pumping station, where it complicated the station's function of dealing with South Idle drainage.

At the Snow Sewer outfall three new 600 mm automatic discharge pumps were installed at the Drainhead station. However, this large watercourse normally discharges by gravity and the pumps are required only at high tide levels. A second pump unit was added in close proximity to deal with the parallel Ferry Drain (known in Vermuyden's time as the Monkham Drain). This augments the older South Axholme IDB pump at this point.

Further pumping capacity became necessary on the Torne at Torne Bridge and Kilham Farm where 250 mm VAF pumps were installed.

These stations are operated under the authority of the Hatfield Chase Corporation. The older New Zealand pumping station in the North Level, discharging into the North Soak Drain, was upgraded at this time to increase its capacity from 1.7 m^3/sec to 2.7 m^3/sec.

The largest new construction was at the Idle outfall at West Stockwith. The new station, opened in 1981, was part of a major scheme to secure flood protection on land at one time (though briefly) owned by Vermuyden and his family and his Dutch colleagues. The installation is the largest all-electric station in the United Kingdom and benefits 8,900 ha (22,000 acres) of farmland and 5,463 ha (13,500 acres) of washland. The four pumps have a combined capacity of 35.4 m^3/sec. Normally the Idle discharges by gravity through a channel incorporated in the station layout. The pumping facility enables the river to cope with flood conditions in times of tidal stress. Most of the recent flooding problems have arisen south of the Idle and outside the Isle of Axholme.

At the same time IDBs have installed new stations, Langholme and Scaftworth (the latter is not marked on Figure 5), adjacent to and discharging into the Idle. The Gringley station will be enlarged.

In the late 1970s and early 1980s Britain's motorway network was considerably extended into Humberside and South Yorkshire. These roads added greatly to the run-off water reaching the drainage systems. Since the area had become a virtual polder all such surplus water required pumping out of the basin. The main burden fell upon the Severn-Trent Authority, although the Yorkshire Water Authority was involved to a lesser extent in the north.[2]

In the centre and south of the area the river authorities took the opportunity of dealing with local problems while providing for the motorway run-off. The following new pumps were installed:

a) Waterton Farm (1977): this set of three 600 mm pumps, each with an output of 0.98 m^3/sec, was located in the area between Hatfield and Armthorpe; a balancing reservoir was incorporated in the system.

b) Low Bank (1977): a similar set of three pumps was installed near the M 180 motorway to deal with run-off and locally accrued water by discharge into the Hatfield Waste Drain.

c) Wood Carr (1978): also located near the M 180 and on the old Sandtoft airfield, a set of three 250 mm pumps was installed to discharge run-off water into the Hatfield Waste Drain.

d) Belton Grange (1979): a small single 250 mm pump was installed with a similar function to Wood Carr and with the same discharge outlet. Additionally, Internal Drainage Boards have installed smaller pumps in the area.

In the north the Black Drain Internal Drainage Board found it necessary to install pumps at each end of the Durham Warping Drain, which discharges into the Don between Thorne and New Bridge. This drain, servicing Dikes Marsh (reclaimed by the Participants) and Moorends (where mining subsidence has occurred), receives M 18 motorway run-off.

Figure 15 illustrates the principal water courses and the larger pumping stations. In their general policy the river authorities at present base their calculations on a steady tidal increase in the Humber of 760 mm per 100 years. This 'secular' rise is a consequence of a lowering in land levels around an axis which passes through Anglesey and Dundee. The River Don is tidal to Doncaster, and in the 1950s the Yorkshire Ouse Catchment Board carried out a scheme which doubled the capacity of the tidal channel through Doncaster to Goole. This greatly reduced the flooding which used to occur regularly in the lower Don. In recent years the run-off from all sources has increased. As a result water authorities have undertaken further flood prevention works to absorb fluvial excesses. The Yorkshire Water Authority works involved embanking all available washlands upstream of Doncaster in order to bring them under control and to gain more efficient use. It is now possible to delay flooding the washes until a critical level in the river is reached. At this point surplus water upstream can be released and so relieve the pressure on the banks through Doncaster.

Notes

1. Personal communication, Severn-Trent Water Authority.
2. Personal communication, Yorkshire Water Authority.

Figure 15 Modern drainage

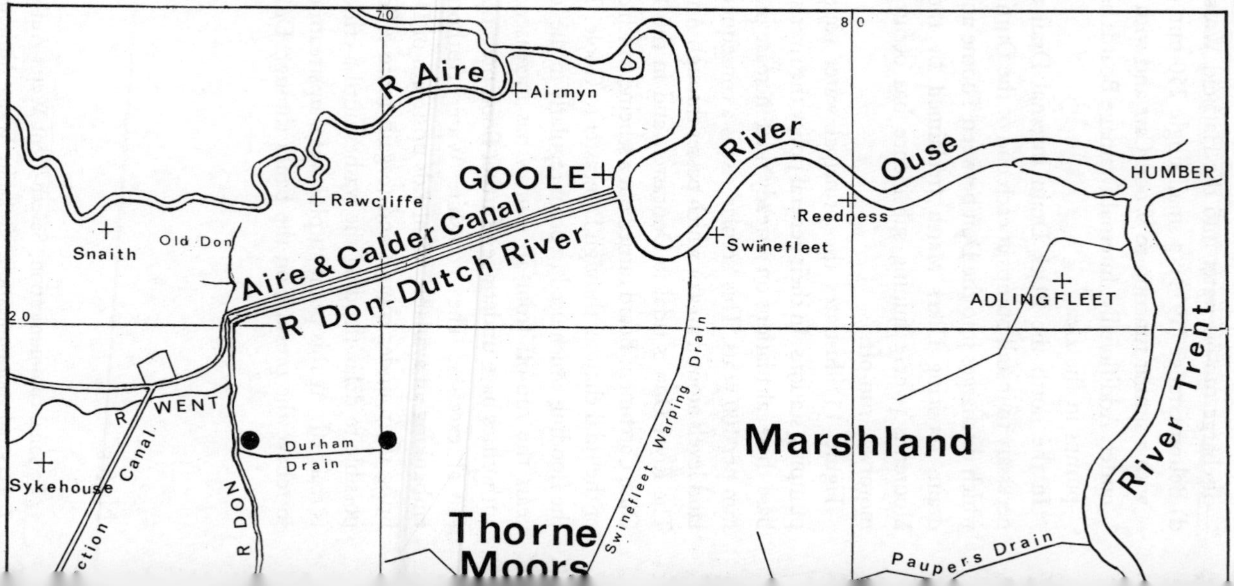

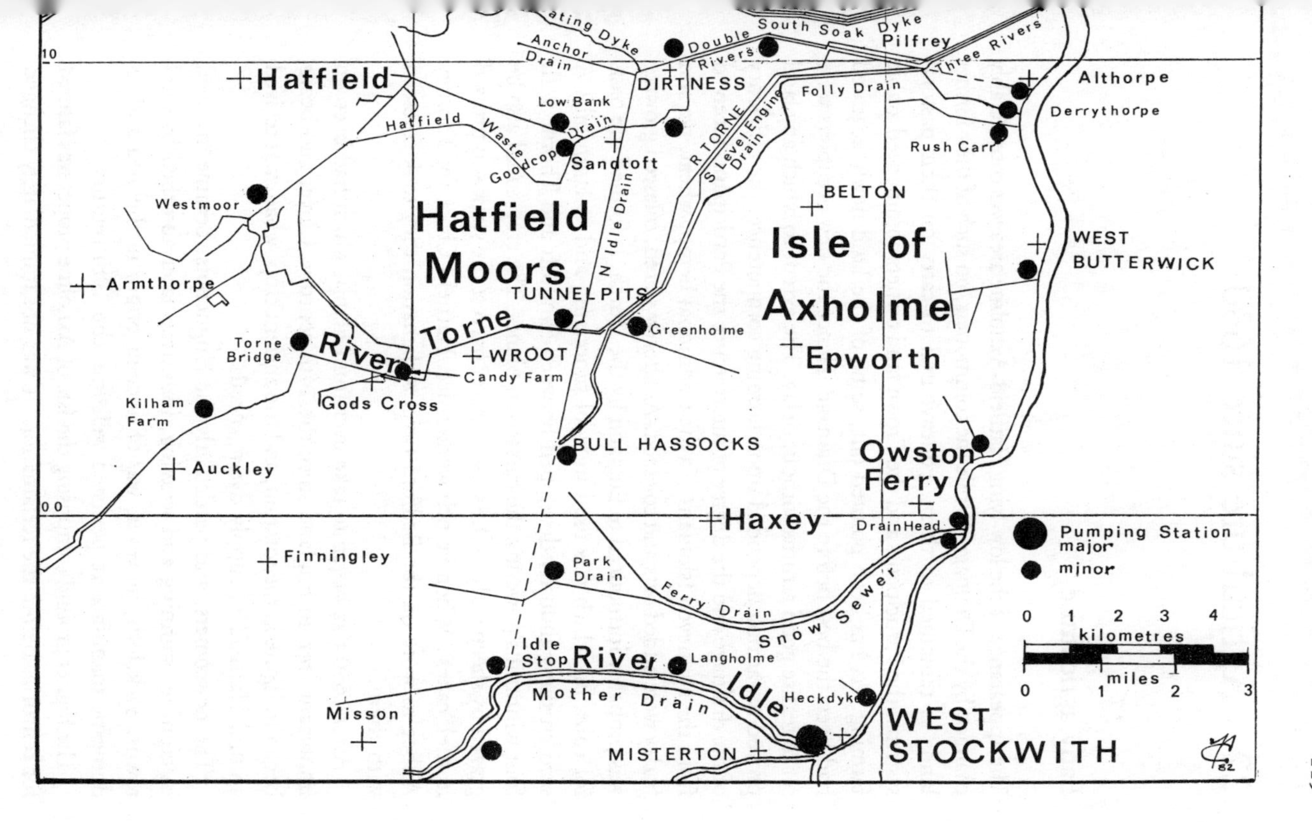
Hatfield
Hatfield Moors
Isle of Axholme
Epworth
BELTON
WEST BUTTERWICK
Althorpe
Derrythorpe
Rush Carr
Three Rivers
Pilfrey
South Soak Dyke
Double Rivers
Folly Drain
DIRTNESS
R TORNE
S Level Engine Drain
Anchor Drain
Low Bank
Drain
Sandtoft
N Idle Drain
TUNNELPITS
Greenholme
Hatfield Waste
Goodcop
WROOT
Candy Farm
River Torne
Gods Cross
Torne Bridge
Westmoor
Armthorpe
Auckley
Kilham Farm
Finningley
BULL HASSOCKS
Owston Ferry
Haxey
DrainHead
Snow Sewer
Ferry Drain
Park Drain
Langholme
Heckdyke
Idle Stop
River Idle
Mother Drain
MISTERTON
WEST STOCKWITH
Misson
Pumping Station
major
minor
0 1 2 3 4
kilometres
miles
0 1 2 3
10
00

22 Agriculture since 1630

Early agriculture

The appearance of the low-lying Hatfield-Axholme area was considerably changed by the Drainage. While the commoners, on such of their former lands as remained to them, endeavoured to carry on their pastoral systems, the Participants and the Crown land owners commenced arable farming. As has been pointed out, some of the land newly acquired had been the best before the Drainage. Hence the new occupiers were set to realise good returns without delay. The extent to which any land proved rewarding depended upon farming competence, the efficiency of the drainage and the degree of interference the Participants received from the aggrieved Islonians. To the traditional hemp, wheat, rye and barley were added oats and coleseed. As already stated, coleseed growing was probably introduced to England by the Dutch. It formed the basis for colza oil which was used in wool processing and as lamp oil.[1] A seed crushing industry developed between Sandtoft and Thorne with four windmills powering the extraction plants. The crop could also be grazed by sheep early in the season. After harvest the straw was utilised in fuel 'cakes'. When French workers left Hatfield Chace for Thorney Abbey to work on the Bedford Level reclamation they took coleseed with them.

After 1630 flax began to take over from hemp, which had been an important crop in England since the 14th century. Clover and beans began to figure in the rotation, and the ancient crop, woad, was revived around Hatfield to supply dyeing needs.

The newcomers, and particularly the Huguenots, became involved in tanning, spinning and weaving, industries later absorbed by local towns. Sackcloth, however, was of ancient origin in the area and its domestic manufacture persisted well into the 19th century.

The higher ground comprising the Isle of Axholme proper was farmed for centuries before the reclamation. It was not immediately changed by Vermuyden's Drainage. A rotation of hemp-barley-hemp-rye without fallows was reported in the Manor of Epworth during the reign of Charles I. On enclosed demesne land an alternate husbandry system of hay, grazing and arable crops was operated including barley, rye, oats, wheat, peas, beans and flax. Barley was the most important crop on the Isle, accounting for a third of the tillage acreage. Wheat, peas and rye followed in order of importance.

As we have seen, farming success eluded the Participants. They failed to realise quick returns and were unable to meet the financial commitments to their Dutch backers. They defaulted on their 'scots' (drainage rates) and within a few years most had given up their holdings and left the country.

The effect of the Drainage upon the commons was immediate and severe.[2] The Manor of Epworth lost 3,200 ha (7,900 acres) and Crowle over 600 ha (1,500 acres) and losses were repeated throughout the area. The stock owners had to reduce numbers and to try to find alternative grazing and fodder. They lost drinking water for their stock in some places and in others suffered flooding of formerly dry pastures. Fishing and fowling were early victims and so also was the natural warping from winter floods.

Very little agricultural progress took place in the area during the long period which preceded the Enclosures, the first of which involved Snaith, Cowick and Rawcliffe in 1754. Farming wet land in the Chace posed a constant struggle, while in the uplands no innovations followed those already mentioned. The Industrial Revolution increased the demand for food supplies which necessitated a better distribution of land.[3] Enclosure Acts enabled these improvements to be started and after the first, in 1754, there followed:

1757	Whitgift Pasture
1760	Reedness, Swinefleet
1779	Amcotts
1781	Snaith, Cowick (open field and meadow)
1795	Parts of Owston, Haxey, Epworth, Belton (4,856 ha, 12,000 acres)
1799-1801	Epworth
1801	Reedness, Swinefleet Moors.

Objections based on the old Mowbray Award were raised in relation to the 1795 Act, but they were overruled. What is more, the Participants benefited from the action of the Commissioners of Enclosures who cut drains on any land necessary to comply with the Acts. Thus common drains were used for warping Participants' land at the commoners' expense.

Of great interest is the survival of the open fields of Epworth and Belton through the whole period of the Enclosures up to the present day. From earliest times the farmers of Epworth possessed a right to fence and enclose an accumulated plot of 2-2.5 ha (5-6 acres).[4] In doing so rights of common were lost but the land could be grazed in common by cattle after harvest. Despite this facility very few such enclosures appear to have been made.

The main Epworth Enclosure Acts were introduced and carried out between 1799 and 1801 but they were applied to the commons and wastes. The land surrounding the villages which were in the open-field system escaped. The reason for this was simply that the necessary majority of 75 per cent of the freehold occupiers consenting to the enclosure could not be obtained. Despite the disapproval of Arthur Young, the great campaigner for enclosures, four of the villages of the Isle (Epworth, Belton, Haxey and Owston), in part, shared with Laxton in Nottinghamshire and a few other places the privilege of retaining the medieval field layout.[5] In Epworth there were four fields: Ellers, Church, East and South. These were divided into smaller strips, known as selions. With the pressure of a growing population the rotation of crops was stretched from three-course to four-course. By common consent the agricultural improvements of the early 19th century were incorporated into the ancient system. Up to 1850 all the occupiers planted the same crop in the same field, even though some 1,587 strips were involved! At that date the medieval common rights of pasture were revoked, permitting the occupier to complete a year-round cultivation plan for his land. The preservation of the fields in this way was a main factor in securing an almost classical nucleated structure for the villages of Epworth and Belton.

Furthermore, the fixed land pattern was responsible for a farming evolution which differed from that of the rest of the county of

Lincoln.[6] The strips tended to increase in size and thus become fewer following sales and exchanges of selions. The total area has also declined. Nevertheless, the system remains distinctive and is clearly shown by aerial photography.

By the late 19th century farms in the Isle of Axholme were smaller generally than those in Marshland and in the Chace proper (Table 7).

Table 7 Average farm size, 1871

District		Hectares (approximate)	Acres
Axholme:	Althorpe	23	56.6
	Belton	31	76.8
	Epworth	36	88.4
Marshland and Levels:	Amcotts	62	153.1
	Garthorpe/Luddington	45	111.5
	Wroot	55	135.2

As we have seen, warping was a condition of later enclosures and in many cases fertility of the land seems to have been greatly improved. The crop chiefly benefiting from this treatment was the potato. When potatoes became a staple of human diet (they were at first fed to horses!) the area grown greatly increased in the Levels, in Marshland and in the Isle of Axholme. In this respect the area preceded the Holland, Lincolnshire, district by many years. Its advantages were mainly associated with excellent river and canal facilities before the main development of railways. Ware potatoes were shipped from Trentside ports via the Humber to London markets, while inland industrial cities were supplied by the canal system westwards. Seed potatoes were a by-product exported to adjacent counties. Local expertise in this crop was considerable and the potato breeder, Findlay, bred the famous 'Up-to-Date' variety at Haxey in the early 1890s.

Wheat and potatoes were often grown alternately, though beans were inserted when soil exhaustion was feared. The vulnerability of such a system to the attacks of the cyst eelworm was not to be realised until well into the 20th century. The scales of advantage were turned in about 1870 when the silt soils of the Boston area were developed for the crop, and the production from Axholme and its district declined.

Hemp growing had ceased by 1839 and with it the famous Gainsborough Hemp Market. In its place flax was extensively grown, the crop being sown in May and pulled at the end of June. Retting took place on the farm and linen was processed locally. At the beginning of the 20th century there was still a 'line' mill at Crowle.

The Axholme parishes were notable for their inherent conservatism and new ideas were accepted only slowly.[7] Few outsiders acquired farms in the Isle, and the tight open-field system was not conducive to drastic change. Late in the 19th century the district's potential for market garden production was aroused, it is said, by a Yorkshireman's initiative. Carrots were found suitable for the blowing sandland near Haxey. Elsewhere onions were successfully introduced. Turnip seed growing was taken up by some farmers, the crop being raised from autumn transplants. However, it was for its celery crop that the Isle of Axholme became famous before the First World War. The blanched celery was well suited to the peats, and pink celery was grown on the warps. In 1911 Blaides of Epworth was growing 40 ha (100 acres) of this crop on a market garden holding of 240 ha (600 acres). Celery was often intercropped with potatoes. Fertilisers for these demanding crops were obtained from organic and inorganic sources. Stable manure, fish and bones were obtained from Hull, Doncaster, Grimsby and even London, while superphosphates, sulphate of ammonia and potash were supplied by chemical firms. The local product, alabaster or gypsum, was employed both as a conditioner and in mixtures with dissolved bones. Red beetroot, important in the Isle today, does not appear to have been grown on a field scale before 1918.

There was a marked reduction in corn growing in the 40 years preceding 1914 and a corresponding increase in land sown down to permanent grass. Though grazing livestock was always part of the upland farming scene there was an increase in grazing stock in this period of arable retrenchment.

With the survival of the medieval field system land tenure and management in the central Isle of Axholme differed markedly from the rest of Lincolnshire. The demand for land was constant and the existence of the selions provided the first rung in the farming ladder for many a new entrant. In the 19th century in particular, such land could only be purchased and the method most commonly employed was that of raising mortgage loans. In times of farming depression interest rates proved to be a considerable burden and livings could be earned only by stringent economies. Indeed it was felt by many small farmers that hired employment would be a preferable source of income. In fact, many took this course and joined the staff of the largest undertakings. In the case of others great pressure was exerted on family members for their unpaid help. When hired assistance became vital it was female labour which was used. It is known that women would often neglect their children for such work. A Crowle doctor recorded that some mothers left infants for the whole day, giving them 'Godfrey's Cordial' (based on opium) to keep them quiet![8]

According to Stonehouse, writing in the late 1830s, the best land on the higher parts of the Isle was worth from £200-£250 per ha (£80-£100 per acre) and rents were from £3.70-£7.50 per ha (£1.50-£3 per acre).[9] Land in the basin of the Chace was certainly much less valuable, though details are obscure. By the mid 1850s unwarped land was clearly at a discount compared with treated areas. In the 1870s land on the open fields was fetching £320 per ha (£130 per acre), 'good' land was worth £300 per ha (£120 per acre) and 'poor', £150 per ha (£60 per acre). There was some decline in values in the late 1890s but a revival in farming fortunes produced higher prices in the early years of the 20th century.

Though standards of husbandry on the intensive farms appear to have been good, on most holdings cultivations and other operations were not efficiently conducted in the Isle of Axholme. Haresign, dealing with the period 1870-1914, alludes to such shortcomings, some of which were attributable to the fragmentation of holdings.[10] Shortage of capital was a further factor, even more acute for owner-occupiers than for tenants. He also blames a considerable number of the natives for a lack of enterprise, energy and zeal!

Modern Agriculture

The whole of the Hatfield-Axholme area may be considered a part of the predominantly arable farming area of eastern England.[11] Even if the less intensely ploughed parishes of Fishlake, Fenwick, Kirk Bramwith and Sykehouse are included, 85 per cent of all the farmed land is arable cropped. Farms in the Isle of Axholme and in Marshland (the northern part of the land lying between the Don, Ouse and Trent) contain almost no permanent grassland. In the central area, including the parishes of Hatfield, Stainforth, Thorne and Finningley, tillage land is scarcely less dominant. The main type of crop comprises cereals, which account for 60-90 per cent of the arable area. Of these cereals only wheat and barley are significant. Amongst other arable crops potatoes are important, being grown in fairly large blocks and with production almost entirely mechanised. The lighter soils of the Isle and of the area east of Doncaster attract the largest concentrations of potato growing but the intensity seldom exceeds 8 per cent of the arable break. Sugar beet is somewhat more widely grown, being favoured by factories in York, Brigg and Newark. Oilseed rape, which, as has been stated, probably owed its introduction to the foreign settlers of Hatfield Chace, has enjoyed a return to favour in recent years. The yellow brilliance of the scattered fields colour the region in May and the crop itself forms a useful addition to the restricted range of modern systems.

No crop is more identified with the Isle of Axholme than red beetroot. Of fairly recent introduction, the crop achieves a desirable blend of size and yield in the lower levels of Epworth, Haxey, Owston Ferry and Wroot. In 1982 Wroot parish devoted a remarkable 22 per cent of its arable area to the crop, a concentration scarcely equalled throughout England.[12] Today, few vegetables other than peas are grown, and these mainly by specialists. Peas are associated with the Marshland parishes, although there are smaller concentrations in Epworth, Haxey and

Table 8 Modern farm systems, 1981 (in hectares)

	Don-Went Area	Hatfield-Thorne	Central Axholme	Marshland
	Fishlake Fenwick Kirk Bramwith Sykehouse	Hatfield Stainforth Thorne Finningley	Epworth Haxey Owston Wroot	Amcotts Crowle Eastoft Garthorpe Luddington Reedness Swinefleet Ousefleet
Farm area	3,292	8,946	7,891	9,526
Crops	1,158	7,556	7,123	9,095
Crops (%)	35	84	90	95
Cereals	997	5,538	4,312	6,625
Cereals as % of farm	30	62	55	69
Vegetables	11	547	1,352	1,002
Dairy cows	729	429	357	14
Sheep	948	1,209	172	0

Source: Ministry of Agriculture, Fisheries and Food

Owston Ferry.

The arable areas carry very few grazing stock, whole parishes returning not a single head of either cattle or sheep. Large specialist pig and poultry units are found but these are unrelated to field systems.

The Fishlake-Sykehouse area provides a most interesting contrast with the rest of the region. In the Middle Ages its land was considered more valuable than that to the east and south. Today the heavy soils of this district prove difficult to manage even with modern equipment. Poor drainage has greatly limited arable crops and has persuaded many farmers to concentrate on dairying enterprises. To what extent can Vermuyden be blamed for modern shortcomings? It must be remembered that the artificial nature of the lower Don (see Chapter

3) may have impaired land drainage to the west. It was certainly not undertaken to assist Fishlake and Sykehouse. Vermuyden's work of embanking the south and east sides of the Don produced a major hostile reaction from the local inhabitants. However, they appeared to have been well pleased by the subsequent cutting of Dutch River. One could conclude that the soil characteristics betoken a much lower potential than elsewhere and that the farming systems developed represent an acceptable compromise between arable and stock farming.

The great difference in the human condition since the 17th century is the decrease in people who owe their livelihood to agriculture. About half of the farms of Hatfield and Axholme are classed as 'part-time', but the average size is about 55 ha (136 acres) (Table 8). Almost all field and barn operations are mechanised and the entire farm team averages little more than three per holding.

Notes

1. Wells, S., *The History of the Drainage of the Great Level of the Fens called Bedford Level* (1830); and Blith, W. (1652), op. cit., Chapter 9.
2. Thirsk, J. (1957), op. cit.
3. Slater, G., *The English Peasantry and the Enclosures of Common Fields* (Constable, 1907); and Brown, R., *A General View of the Agriculture of the West Riding* (Board of Agriculture, 1793-1812).
4. Crompton, P.A., 'Epworth, Some Aspects of its Evolving Landscape' (Thesis, Padgate College of Higher Education, 1977).
5. Young, A. (1770), op. cit.
6. Haresign, S.R., 'Agricultural Change and Rural Society in the Lincolnshire Fenlands and the Isle of Axholme 1870-1914' (PhD Thesis, University of East Anglia, 1980).
7. Ibid.
8. Ibid.
9. Stonehouse, W.B. (1839), op. cit.
10. Haresign, S.R. (1980), op. cit.
11. Ministry of Agriculture, Fisheries and Food, Statistics 1981.
12. Ibid.

23 Wildlife since the Drainage

References to natural history during the period of the Drainage are rare and of dubious accuracy. Stonehouse's account written 200 years after the Drainage is the first to give any information on the subject.[1]

Fish

It is known from ancient documents that fisheries existed and were diverse. As elsewhere in marshy and coastal areas eels were not only a staple of food but were used as a form of currency. Stonehouse reported salmon, sturgeon and smelt in the Trent, although salmon numbers were apparently declining.[2] Porpoises had been known to pursue fish up the Trent. Howes also provides details of fish species in the area of the Chace.[3]

Birds

Stonehouse gives useful information on the birds of the area in his time. Cranes, storks, egrets and night herons had become extinct. It is known that the crane bred in Britain in the 16th century, but there is doubt as to whether the night heron ever did so. Storks and egrets have almost certainly never bred in Britain. Stonehouse states that herons were numerous and that bitterns were not rare, he himself having shot two in 1817. He records gerfalcons (usually regarded as very rare in Britain), 'moor buzzards' (hen harriers) at Lindholme and the ruff. He states that the ruff was 'seldom met with', which is hardly surprising as it was being snared and fattened for the London market in some quantity. Snipe numbers were also smaller than formerly, perhaps for a similar reason. Stonehouse confirms the fairly common species of mallard, scaup, shelduck, pintail and pochard. He also refers to the 'swallow-tailed shelduck' (long-tailed duck), which was almost certainly not a breeder.

The Dutch brought not only their drainage skills to Hatfield Chace but also their knowledge of 'harvesting' wild ducks in decoys.[4] In earlier times in England decoys had been employed in the corners of large meres to catch flightless ducks. The birds were driven into tunnel-like nets ('pipes') and trapped. One such well-known decoy was at Crowle. In the Dutch method, which was applicable to the partly drained land of the Chace, a near circular pool was adapted or specially constructed for the purpose. Approximately 1 ha (2.5 acres) in extent, it employed tame decoys to attract a resident but growing population of ducks from the summer onwards. Camouflaged pipes radiating from around the perimeter were arranged with narrowing extremities. The key to the operation lay in the tame decoys which were accustomed to paddle up the pipes. Wild ducks were attracted by hemp seed which was spread at the pipe entrances and they then followed the tame decoys to the end of the pipes. The first Dutch decoys were in the vicinity of Thorne Moors and others were constructed later. An unusually large concentration of at least six were located around Crowle, indicating the favourable nature of the countryside for the main species of wild duck. The sites of some decoys are known, but most disappeared after the decline of the practice around the mid-19th century. The design and principles of the method were adopted very generally in England, Wales and Ireland and around 250 decoys were in operation at one time.

The mute swan, indigenous to Europe, at one time formed an important source of food in England.[5] This would certainly have applied to the Hatfield-Axholme area. Partial domestication became general before 1186 and, presumably because of relative scarcity, possession of individual birds or 'games' of swans became a subject for licence. Royal games were kept on the Thames and the Avon, while commoners and other organisations such as religious houses were granted permits to own birds. Such birds, usually pinioned, were required to be marked on the bill with a registered distinguishing mark known as a 'cygninota'. Oversight of all such swans was provided by a Royal Swanherd who was represented in each county. All unmarked swans were automatically royal property. Before the introduction of the turkey in the 16th century swan was the traditional Christmas meat.

In Hatfield Chace the number of swans appears to have declined from 1626, not necessarily by reason of the Drainage. Perhaps because of the royal interest Hatfield retained a strong control over the birds by way of swan records and a Swanmote Court. There was a Proclamation of Hatfield in 1547 establishing swanniers' regulations. A number of swan ponds were retained in the Chace after the Drainage and when Cornelius Vermuyden purchased The Manor he became a swan owner.

The 18th century saw a decline in the close control of swans, apart from the 'upping' or marking by particular guilds on the Thames. Although Bewick, in 1800, recorded seeing 'swans without an owner' on the Trent, Stonehouse reported that in his time (up to 1835) both tame and wild swans had disappeared. It is difficult to account for this dramatic fall in numbers. In any case, corroboration for the statement is wanting. Certainly, today the mute swan is not rare on the rivers and dykes of the area. Furthermore, both Bewick and Whooper swans are known and are believed to have overwintered in the past.

The Hatfield-Axholme area presents an interesting range of wildlife well adapted to the local habitats. These habitats include unreclaimed peat and intensive arable farming on fenland and upland. Both local and national organisations maintain reserves and a great deal of observation and study is constantly being carried out. The Royal Society for the Protection of Birds owns a site at Blacktoft near the Ouse-Trent confluence. The Lincolnshire (South Humberside) Country Trust operates seven reserves in the Isle of Axholme. Perhaps the most interesting of these is Epworth Turbary, an area of some 34 ha and a former raised bog. The peat, now a mere 25 cm deep has almost dried out and much has become wooded. Wetter sections are being encouraged and there is some resurgence of *Sphagnum*. The turbary supports an unusually large concentration of various members of the crow family. The lakes at Lindholme and Crowle are noteworthy resorts of ducks and other waterfowl. Another of the Axholme reserves is located at Haxey. Just outside the area, but typifying many of its wetland features, is the Yorkshire Wildlife Trust reserve of Potteric Carr on the headwaters of the Torne. Of the bird species to be found in the area the following groups are of interest:[6]

Falcons *(Falconidae)*
It is pleasing that the marshland species, the hen harrier, still frequents The Levels and may well have nested there. It would undoubtedly have been common in Vermuyden's time, as it was when Stonehouse wrote. The merlin, the sparrow hawk and the hobby falcon also occur, while the kestrel is common and a resident. Ospreys have been reported on passage.
Ducks *(Anatidae)*
Ducks are well represented on the pools and flooded washes, as on the rivers and dykes. Teal, mallard and shoveller are common, while pintail, merganser, goosander, goldeneye, shelduck and gadwall are less frequent, and gargenay rare. Wigeon occur in fairly small numbers and irregularly. Tufted duck and pochard frequent the pools at Crowle and Lindholme. Geese are less common on the ground than in similar areas, though Canada geese breed locally.
Herons *(Ardeidae)*
Herons are common but the bittern has not been reported in recent times.
Waders *(Scolopacidae)*
Many of the small waders are observed in the area. They include greenshank, common and green sandpiper, snipe, woodcock and ruff. The plovers are well represented with the lapwing, ring plover, little ring plover, golden plover and that unpredictable migrant, the dotterel. Oyster catcher and curlew are seen mainly *en route* to coastal marshes. The avocet is known to have bred near the Trent outfall in 1837 but it has yet to stage its reappearance.
Grebes *(Popicipidae)*
Both the great crested and the little grebe frequent the larger areas of water along with the familiar coot and moorhen.

The kingfisher is seen occasionally but is rather uncommon.

Woodlands and shrub-covered areas occur through the levels and on the ridges. With increasing tree cover on Epworth Turbary a wide range of song birds occur. The northern limit of the nightingale is in this region and the bird has frequented Crowle in recent years. Of the other woodland songsters the blackcap, lesser whitethroat, tree pipits, tree creepers, wrens, willow warblers and the turtle dove join most of the familiar species. However, nuthatches and redstarts are rare. Of the tits the willow tit and the long-tailed tit are encountered, but the marsh tit is uncommon. The sedge warbler and the reed warbler are regularly present. On the fields and around ditches yellow wagtails, corn bunting, reed bunting and wheatears are frequently seen, and bramblings are autumn visitors. Green, great and spotted and lesser spotted woodpeckers have been reported.

Of the owls perhaps the long-eared is the most prominent, especially in the neighbourhood of Crowle. Short-eared owls have overwintered and bred on Reed's Island in the Humber. The little owl is also present and the barn owl makes use of old buildings. Hatfield Moors provide a fertile habitat for nightjars.

Insects and Related Forms

Dragon-flies are common and appear to be increasing (the hobby falcon has been taking advantage of this food source). The large heath and brimstone butterflies occur in some localities while oakegger, emperor and fox moths are found on the peat moors. The death's head hawk moth feeds on potato foliage in the levels, and the nye moth is also reported.

Mammals

Roe deer, in small numbers, find cover in the various woodlands, providing a living memory of former times. Foxes are common but the badger is less so. The otter, once numerous, is now virtually extinct.

Reptiles and Amphibia

Grass snakes are found locally in the Isle and adders are particularly common on Crowle Moors. Frogs frequent suitable habitats throughout the levels, and both the common and great crested newt are well known.

Flora

The range of plants in the Hatfield-Axholme area is extensive. The *Orchidaceae* are worthy of special note and the discovery and protection of many species in this fragile family reflect the devotion of local naturalists. The few old unfertilised meadows, some with ridge and furrow, produce some interestingly rare species.

Notes

1. Stonehouse, W.B. (1839), op. cit.
2. Ibid.
3. Howes, C., 'Fish of the Hatfield Chace', *The Naturalist* (1973).
4. Limbert, M., 'The Old Duck Decoys of SE Yorkshire', *The Naturalist*, 103 (1978), pp. 95-103; and an Addendum, *The Naturalist*, 107 (1982), pp. 69-71.
5. Ticehurst, N.F., *The Mute Swan in England* (Cleaver Hulme, 1957).
6. Trinder, G., personal communication (1983).

Bibliography

The dramatic events which began to unfold in the heart of Hatfield Chace in the 1620s entirely lacked a contemporary recorder. Though legal documents survive, the local impact can be judged only from the writings of historians who had no personal contact with the characters.

Dugdale's *History of Imbanking and Draining* (1662) includes useful information regarding the drainage of Hatfield Chace. Much more material was compiled by Abraham de la Pryme in his two works (1696 and *c*. 1698) referred to in Chapter 12. His local background was valuable and to a large extent his account was used by most subsequent national and local authors. George Stovin, of a well-known local family, wrote in 1752 and provided a good background to the effects of the Drainage. Many subsequent authors were of Yorkshire or Lincolnshire origin but incorporated much information already published. Into this category fall Peck (1813), Wainwright (1826), Hunter (1828), Stonehouse (1839), Read (1858), Hatfield (1866) and Tomlinson (1882). Of these, Stonehouse was the most comprehensive in his descriptions.

During the 19th century the literature gradually became more detailed and technically proficient. For instance, important contributions were made by the Huguenot Society of London, whose members studied details of foreign workers in the Chace. Samuel Smiles (1862) included local engineering details, though much of his historical coverage was a repetition of earlier works. An outstanding contribution to the history of pumping machinery was the paper of Gibbs (1887), then a civil engineering student. From the 1770s onwards the subject of agriculture was well covered, notably by Arthur Young and the Board of Agriculture. The Royal Agricultural Society of England played a useful part in its reportage, particularly of the practice of warping.

Much technical and sociological background has been provided in the 20th century. Dunston (1909), a local engineer, is a noteworthy example. The River Authorities have now accumulated much knowledge and experience of the particular problems of the Levels. The work of

Dr Joan Thirsk on the sociological background of the fenland has changed some of the historical concepts of the Drainage and its effects. More recently some outstanding theses have been produced, including those of Metcalfe (1960), Crompton (1977) and Haresign (1980).

An interesting aspect of the literature is the way in which many authors divide sharply as to their approval or their disapproval of the Drainage, revealing a corresponding regard or hatred for the person of Cornelius Vermuyden! Amongst the pro-Vermuyden lobby come Dugdale, de la Pryme, Young, Wainwright, Smiles, Korthals-Altes and Harris. The 'antis' include many with a more local connection: Peck, Stonehouse, Hamilton, Tomlinson, Stovin and Thirsk.

Works of a general nature include the following:

Allen, T., *A New and Complete History of the County of York* (1828).

Anonymous, 'Epworth and Surrounds. A Basis for Local Study' (duplicated, Mechanics Institute, Epworth, 1973).

Bunting, W., Dolby, M.J., Howles, C.A. and Skidmore, P., *Outline Study of Hatfield Chace* (Thorne, private publication, 1969).

Cory, V., *Hatfield Chace and its Reclamation* (Ministry of Agriculture, Fisheries and Food, 1972).

Darby, H. C., *The Medieval Fenland* (Cambridge University Press, 1940).

Hamilton, J. A., *The Manuscript in a Red Box* (1903) (Bodley Head, Fair Books, 1966).

Hamilton, J. A., *Captain John Lister* (Hutchinson, 1906; reprinted by Scholar Press and Mechanics Institute, Epworth, 1978).

Head, G., *A Home Tour through the Manufacturing Districts of England, Summer 1835* (1836).

Holland, D., *Changing Landscapes in South Yorkshire* (private publication, 1980).

Hunter, J., *History and Topography of South Yorkshire* (The Deanery of Doncaster, 1828).

Read, W., *History of the Isle of Axholme, its Manors and Parishes*, Fletcher, T. C. (ed.) (Epworth, 1858).

Taylor, J.S., *Hatfield Chace* (W. M. Darley, Brewers, Thorne, 1960).

Willis, W.R., 'Historic Floods in the Isle of Axholme and Hatfield', *Durdey's Almanack and General Advertiser* (1901).

Index